ETERNAL | LIFE

or

ETERNAL | EXISTENCE

YOUR WILL

by G. F. Standley

Eternal Life or Eternal Existence
Your Will
by G. F. Standley

Printed in the United States of America

ISBN 978-1-60647-843-1

Unless otherwise indicated, Bible quotations are taken from The 1611 King James Version of the Bible.

www.xulonpress.com

WARNING!

This text, "Eternal Life or Eternal Existence—
Your Will," contains graphic descriptions of
inhuman torture of the mind, body and spirit. Do
not read this text if torture, graphic descriptions of
the mind, body and spirit affects you. No words
written within this text refer to the reader, rather to
the author.

TABLE OF CONTENTS

CHAPTER ONE

LANGUAGES, GOD AND MAN

There are more than two hundred spoken languages here on planet earth. If you could put a person of each language in a room to speak, who would be able to understand the other? Within some of these languages are gods, and others no gods at all. One must have faith to believe in God, but it takes more faith to believe there is no God. Whichever you choose, faith is needed.

Having faith that there is no God would be putting yourself as a god. The questions that could be asked of your intelligence, reasoning or anything would go truthfully unanswered. Having faith that you are a god or will become a god someday is a fantasy or a dream of your imagination. What have you done to deserve such an honor?

The purpose of all these languages is quite simple: Different languages when spoken cannot be understood, right? Trying to learn all these languages is an impossible task—yes! All of these languages have one thing in common: They can all communicate and receive the gift from the eternal God of life. That's right! Receiving an eternal gift for something you don't deserve or can't earn is yours for the taking by simply just asking. **Today you need to realize that you are a created spirit being and that is all you ever will be**. You have only one purpose here on earth! It is to have (present-tense) eternal life provided by your creator. Your free will will determine this for you. Without accepting this gift of eternal life, all that you'll ever do is "live" and "live" spelled backwards is "**evil**."

In your own language this eternal, holy, spirit God will be revealed to you. This God is very patient, willing to wait for you. The opportunities you have are many to receive this gift. In times past it has been recorded that some people wait to accept this gift of eternal life from God on their last living day. Others it has been recorded from texts of old day that they wait and wait and wait and do not accept this gift of eternal life from their creator, die and forever live in **eternal existence**.

CHAPTER TWO

PLANETS NAMED FOR GODS

From planet earth looking up into the universe, man has given stars and numerous planets god names. Each of these planets named for a god have one thing in common with the other; that is, they were determined to be gods by man. One would have to ponder, "Why were these planets chosen?" Many other planets are currently being discovered. Are there going to be more gods on the horizon? Questions need to be asked: What decision-making went into deciding which planets are gods and which are not. Having a planet receive the title of god: "What an honor!" How do these god planets relate to the creation of man? When people die, and they do, having faith only in a planet god will create only "**eternal existence**," permanently separated from their creator, a holy, eternal, spirit God.

The planet "gods," shapes, colors, textures, rings, moons and sizes all vary from one another. Their temperatures are not controlled by themselves. They all are not self-sustaining. These planets have no direct communication with the human race. So! Why are there planets named for gods? No one can give a correct answer. To claim that planet gods exist, and they do, which planet god is the one, true God? Do these planet gods know there are other planet gods, too? One should think not and that is the correct answer.

The planet sun god is still worshipped today by a few. The Babylonians of Babylon of old days (thousands of years ago) worshipped the planet sun as their god. This group of people occupied a land area known as modern-day Turkey. Fiery dances, rituals and bloody sacrifices were made to the planet sun god. The Babylonians knew after the worship that the planet sun god was pleased because the sun god gave its light again. Little did the Babylonians know that the planet sun would always shed its light.

Most of the people of the Babylon empire participated in worshiping the planet sun god. Some just watched with amazement the people worshiping this sun god. This government was the author of the planet sun god. "Come here to live and the planet sun god will be your god, too."

The rise and fall of many great empires, like the Babylonians, lasted only for two hundred years (approximately). At such time, the empires fall internally or are taken over by a country nearby. During the completion of the takeover, other gods are introduced to the people or no gods at all.

Many god planets are found in our solar system. Some of these planet gods' names are: Venus, Saturn, Pluto, Earth, and numerous others. The purposes of why "man" chose these planets to be gods are quite simple; the answer being: the god of "planet earth" is trying to convince the human race not to accept the free gift of eternal life from the one, truly, holy, spirit God, the creator of all things material and spiritual.

Why and for what reason is there a god of planet earth is known only to a few. Most others do not know this earth god exists. Where you live on planet earth is where this god is found. On every continent, land, water, and air, this god can travel. He travels faster than the speed of light; can travel back whence he came, where this earth god was created and returned back to earth (within seconds). This earth god has a beginning, an end and a purpose known only to a few.

This planet earth god is a spirit. Much has been written and spoken of about this spirit earth god. A spirit is like the wind. You cannot see the wind where it comest or goest but you know the effects and results of the wind. A spirit is like the same.

You need to know the name and where this planet earth god first lived. To spell the word lived backwards will tell you this god's name and about his character. "Lived" spelled backwards is... **"devil."** Where this god first lived was a spiritual place known only to spirits. This place was designed by a holy, eternal spirit God, creator of all spirits, to be served and honored by this "first set" of angelic spirits.

Long ago before there was day, night or time, there was, and still is, a place where only spirits live with a free will. This free will is the same as yours. Yes! You have a free will. You can pick and choose right from wrong and act upon the same. All these spirits can do the same. These angelic spirits all were created by one, true, holy eternal spirit with only truth prevailing.

A spirit has no body. This is kind of hard to imagine but true. (Remembering a spirit is like the wind.) Spirits cannot sleep, eat, breathe or create anything. Everything is provided for them to exist, travel, reason or communicate. This holy, eternal, spirit God who created these angelic spirits is a jealous eternal God.

Where these angelic spirits lived, and some do still live there today, began quite a spiritual war. This war was between the jealous, holy, true, eternal spiritual God and a created spirit (singular). This created spirit was the most beautiful, intelligent, intellectual created spirit of all. Today this created spirit is known as the god of planet earth and has a name. This name is the devil.

Much has been written about this planet earth god called the devil. The purpose and why this spiritual devil god exists has been told for more than two thousand years. The purpose for this earthly god and for the only purpose for you here for him is to enter eternal existence.

A background check needs to be done with detailed information about this earth god, the devil. Let's start at his place of origin. This earth god spirit was created and resided in a spiritual place where only spirits reside. There was no other spirit that was created better than this one. Smarts, clever, wisdom, knowledge, beauty, wit, charm, communication, intelligence, are brief descriptions of this spirit's creativity. This evil, demonic, earth god spirit knows that he is a created spirit by the one, true, holy, eternal spirit. Back then in this spiritual place, and even now, this earth god spirit has (present tense) direct communication with its creator. At one time this created spirit ruled a portion of this spiritual place. Much authority was given to control, reason, exert love to their holy, eternal, spirit God.

This evil spirit, as part of his created process, was given a free will. A free will governs you to know right from wrong, good from evil, eternal life or eternal existence, then you can act upon the same. This most highly intelligent spirit could convince other spirits to do his wrongs. These evil spirits' goal was to take over this spiritual place, a place known only to angelic spirits. It's not known in exact details the wrongs that were done against their creator. What is known is that one-third of all rebelling, evil spirits were sent out, became "**castaways**" from this spiritual place and were sent here to planet earth. This happening occurred long ago. There is no time in spiritual places, so no dates are provided and are of no importance.

The time clock is now ticking for all these evil spirits before they will (not maybe) enter eternal existence. This spiritual warfare began long ago between the one, true, holy eternal spirit, creator of all things material and spiritual and the most beautiful, intelligent, charming, clever, witty and knowledgeable created spirit. This spiritual war, known only to a few, is and will ever be the longest (earth time-wise) of any war. The action, reaction, the moves, those who are in rank (too many to name), various commands and charges will be; till victory has been proclaimed by this holy, eternal, spirit God.

This spiritual war began where only spirits dwell. This spiritual war has entered planet earth and will return from whence it began. At this time of returning, the defeated spirits will be sentenced for their crimes. The place of sentencing will be eternal existence, where there is "wailing and gnashing of teeth," while embedded in a lake of fire 24/7. The spiritual battle currently lags on.

The purpose of this most beautiful, intelligent, evil spirit (who knows you by name) and (all the weak areas of your life) is to try and capture your spirit to eternal existence. This place is for those one-third rebelling angelic spirits, when time will be no more. In this physical place there is pain beyond comprehension, burning flames of torture, smog, coughing 24/7, skin rashes, and being totally separated from their creator forever. This will occur for those who rebel against their creator, the holy, eternal, spiritual God, when this spiritual war is over.

A true story unfolds at this time to describe in graphic detail what this evil spirit wants of you. This evil spirit, the devil, has captured many spirits from planet earth. You need to know this! **You are a spirit. You will always be a spirit. You were born a spirit. You will die a spirit. <u>You are a spirit that has temporarily taken on a human body</u>**. An eternal, holy spirit created you a spirit for his honor and glory to have (present tense) an eternal life relationship with you. Your spirit controls you. Your body will soon decay, completely stop functioning in about (three score plus 10) years from the day you were born. This is true for the entire human race. The common thread of all people of all generations is that death occurs and the body goes back into the earth (from whence it came).

The devil (the god of planet earth), which is a created supernatural, beautiful spirit, has only the ability to influence you to do evil. His skillful tactics are to have you believe that evil things are good, and good things evil. This demonic, evil spirit, when his journey through time and space is over, will enter eternal existence. This place, already created, has endless existence, ultimate pain and suffering of the mind, body and spirit, fiery flames of heat scorching the body and total mind control of your thoughts of why those are there.

This evil spirit can capture you, and is trying to do this, twenty-four/seven. This spirit does not sleep or eat, or rest. Its only mission here on planet earth is to provide a one-way path to enter eternal existence. Only upon your death, if your "free will" chooses to follow this demonic, evil path, then you're captured in eternal existence where there are worms that feed upon those who dwell there.

A graphic detailed story which did occur (several thousand years ago) and has been told more times than most stories: This evil, demonic, planet earth god captured a man on planet earth who, upon his death (within a blink of an eye) entered eternal existence. This is a true story (an actual happening). To define the word "captured" would be that there is no way out. Once you're captured, there is no hope to leave. This would be the best example of "how" and "why" eternal existence begins.

Over a thousand years ago (the exact date is not recorded), there was a man of great wealth. The people who lived nearby knew he was wealthy. His house was an example of his wealth. Gates were around the house so no one could enter or leave without the knowledge of this man. There were beggars who came on the outside of the gates begging to be fed from the crumbs of the rich man's table. People saw the rich man wear fine linen clothing and jewelry, which showed off his wealth.

Not much is known about his schooling, his work or his activities that led up to his riches. He was so rich that the food from his table was thrown out beyond the gates so that the beggars might be fed. This man ate, slept and talked about his wealth. The evil spirit (knew him by name) was watching to slowly capture him toward the entrance of eternal existence.

He had five brothers who knew of his wealth. There was a time in this rich man's life to receive the gift of eternal life as others did receive it, and enter eternal life. The rich man's "free will" chose not to receive the gift of eternal life but rather chose the broad road of eternal existence.

For it is written, "**Once you die, then the judgment**." The rich man died, his body and spirit were captured by the evil planet earth god, "the devil." He has now entered eternal existence.

The rich man describes the following of his captivity: Eternal existence is place of total darkness with no light to observe your surroundings. Fiery flames with extreme high temperatures, possibly hotter than the flames of planet sun. His skin was burning slowly. Trying to completely understand this description from this rich man's story is difficult from an earthly perspective because at eternal existence there are no set of laws, only boundaries.

The rich man's first response was to remember his past. His memory was well intact (no memory loss). His thoughts of his past were: his great wealth, servants, guards, beggars begging for food at his gates. His senses were working, as he could see, feel hunger, thirst, hear and think.

Being in torment at his arrival, he thirsted for water to cool the tip of his tongue. The rich man talked and remembered his servants on planet earth who would give into his every command. No water or his servants were found, here at his new setting.

On his short arrival he could see and visualize from afar others he knew on planet earth. These others also died but entered eternal life. He noticed one of them, who was a beggar, who used to come to his earthly home to beg for food on the outside of his gates. He yelled and called the beggar by name, "Come here and give me a drink to cool me down!" A voice answered and said... "No!"

A brief conversation took place between the rich man who entered eternal existence, from a voice of afar in eternal life. Your "free will" decided your fate. Although you were rich with earthly possessions, you did not accept the free gift of eternal life. **This gift was yours for the taking, by just asking**. Patience is a virtue that expired upon your death. Here you are being tormented for eternity, in total darkness with fire and brimstone burning at temperatures that cannot be recorded.

Your memory is well intact, as you are calling out for one of your beggars. Your beggar received the "gift" of eternal life while he was living on planet earth. He died and now he is with "Me" in eternal life. He cannot hear you, think about you, or give into your commands anymore. Now he is comforted and you are forever tormented in eternal existence. Between us and you is a great gulf as far as the east is from the west. One cannot pass through or travel from the other. "**Let's make a deal**," inquires the rich man. The rich man tried to "make a deal" with the voice at eternal life. Let me go back and tell my five brothers about eternal existence. Surely if one came back from the dead, others would repent and believe! A final reply was given to the rich man. "No one would believe if one returns from the dead." They, on planet earth (human race only), have their "free will" to believe or not believe.

Eternal existence from an earthly perspective would be to say: mind, body and spirit tormented forever. Imagine a hot day while walking barefoot on a hot tar road. Ouch! Your hot feet slowly burning. To rapidly walk off the hot scorching tar road to cool your feet would be reasonable, right? Touching a hot frying pan on the stove would cause you to release the pan to then cool your hand in water, right? What a relief? The burning hand is now being comforted. You're running a race, your heart is rapidly beating, there's perspiration covering your body; now's the time for a cool drink, food for the body... Ah! What relief! But... at eternal existence there is no food, drink or rest... just severe pains of torture.

The hot temperature of planet sun is beaming down on your skin. Your skin burns, wriggles with unbearable pains. Lotion on your skin and keeping out of the hot sun equals a quick fix for your ailment, right? At eternal existence there are no remedies or quick fixes... just decaying of the body. At eternal existence the rich man's body and spirit are united as if they never departed. In a blink of an eye of his earthly death he entered and was captured in eternal existence by this earth god known as the devil. From the rich man's own testimony he does have his senses, mind, body, spirit, eyes, ears, nose and thirst for a drink. His torments of his mind, body and spirit continue from his entry of eternal existence to this present day.

CHAPTER THREE

ANIMAL GODS

A nimal gods have been and still are worshipped as gods on all of the continents of planet earth. From the far east to the far west, animal gods are what some people believe to be their god. Some of these animal gods are living, dead, or have been molded from gold, silver, marble or other precious metals to be worshipped for their image. The image of these animal gods is usually at the entrance place of worship. Prior to the people entering, a ritual or ceremony would take place. This would be to honor the animal god before the worship began. Not much written information is known when the animal gods first came to be worshipped; or did man come first? Whichever is believed, animal gods are still worshipped.

The North American buffalo is praised, glorified and worshipped as an animal god by some of the Indian tribes. Globally, other Indian tribes have other animal gods to worship. In North America, the buffalo god is the most popular god. The male buffalo receives the title of god, although no clear information is found as to why the female wasn't chosen.

The chants, clapping of hands, whistles blowing, beating of drums, best describe the rituals and ceremonies to the buffalo god. Many Indian tribes have gone to war among the different tribes to gain control over the buffalo god. These wars were to settle land rights, marriages, or which tribe controls the other. Since there are no laws, texts or any other evidence of truth found about the buffalo god, this animal god goes unchallenged to its purpose. These tribal wars have gone on for centuries, even to this very date in history, with no end in sight. The North American Indians have petitioned the United States Government... and won!... not to hunt to kill the buffalo. Their second petition... and won!... to engrave the buffalo on an American coin.

The Indian tribes have other animal gods to worship. Each tribe varies the rituals and ceremonies to worship the buffalo god. Which buffalo god rules over the other? One can only ponder (not known). Disputes and wars among the Indian tribes occurred since the beginning of time when they placed their faith in the animal god called the buffalo. Having faith in the animal god called the buffalo will place one on a broad road of destruction. Upon the death of their earth life they will enter eternal existence. For it is written, "Man shall rule over the animals of planet earth," not the animals governing man.

The elephant god is found mostly in hot, humid jungles where there is no rule of law. Elephants go through many rituals of strength, size and ability to stand still for moments of time to determine which elephant receives the title of god from the people who dwell there. This place of happening is found mostly in third world countries where the people have no law to govern themselves. Elephant statues made from some of the most precious metals are found at the entrance of the place of worship. Drums drumming, people chanting, music playing and a variety of rituals are performed to honor the elephant god. Nothing is known on how, why or for what purpose the elephant god provides to man and his only purpose in life. What is known only of the elephant god is that the human race has chosen to worship this animal as a god.

The animal known as the dragon is a god worshipped mostly in the Orient. The dragon of the land, air and water is an animal god that travels with speed and does not stop to rest to be worshipped. Knowing this, the images of the dragon god are formed and molded together from metals like gold, silver, rubies and diamonds, so the people can see an image while the worshipping takes place. Open areas where the molded dragon god is placed, people gather to worship this god. Myths say, "Placing a dragon statue at the entrance of the village will protect the people within." This myth has been proved wrong till this day in history. In this ancient world of worshipping the dragon god, each separate village has their different dragon god, too. One could ponder which dragon god is the correct god to worship? Is there one dragon god that has a personal, direct relationship with man? Answer... no! How many animal gods are there? Why are some animals called gods and some are not? The answers are unknown! These animals all die, without a resurrection and return to the earth. For it is written of old day, "Have no other god before Me."

CHAPTER FOUR

A MAN CLAIMS
TO BE GOD

A man who claimed to be God was an actual happening. More than two thousands years ago, there was a man who claimed to be God. Prior to this time, God was only known by his voice. When God spoke to man in the beginning, and over centuries of time, curious man spoke back. Most of these conversations occur when man needed something or when God wanted his truths to be known. God only has influence for you to do good. God's influence to do truths in your life is the only purpose of your creation.

God's voice was known only to a few people. They who heard it recorded in their writings the conversations that took place. The voice of God is similar to the voice you have. Each time God spoke, people listened, sometimes spoke back and an important truth was known at that moment in history.

This man who claims to be God came into this world the usual way. There were a few people who knew of his birth prior to Him being born. A special illuminating light from the east, and from the closest stars, guided those followers to where He was to be born. These followers witness His birth then spread this news afar to many. Communications of this news was by way of mouth of this miracle event.

The early years of His life much is not known. His childhood, friends, the schools He attended, the places He might have lived are not of record and are (not important). The important "good news" of why He was born was told prior to His birth, at His birth, during His lifetime and up to this present day of history, "His story is still being told."

From the day He could speak, till the last words He spoke, people listened. Very early in His youth, elders would ask Him questions and the correct answers He gave were astonishing!

The town folk and elders marveled at the truthful answers of this young man. "**This man knows everything but did not have to learn anything,**" was often quoted by His followers.

In His early years (teenage years) when visiting places of worship, He would give speeches about life and His truths. A crowd would gather to listen as He quoted specific dates and times of history. The rulers, government officials, and those who were in charge of high places would ask "tricky" questions that they thought only they knew. When this young lad responded with the correct answers, they all were amazed! At such a young age (although no age is known), how could He receive such knowledge of accuracy. His name and this event was rapidly spread throughout the land.

He continued traveling to local towns, villages, and people He met along the way, giving more speeches. His closest followers He gave them instructions to do the same. At this time of history (a few thousand years ago), this young lad grew up to be a man that became the most popular person, even to this very day. His life travels (in distances) were only about one hundred miles (only estimating) but His truths, instructions by others have reached distances of around the world on all bodies of water and land. Planet earth's land area He traveled, compared to the total miles of planet earth is huge, yet His writings, truths and popularity are still being taught today.

On an occasion when entering a place of worship, He found gamblers, people betting money to make money, illegal money exchanging. This drew His temper high. Lifting the tables, chairs and watching the scattering of money on the ground He began to speak: "A place to worship God is not to have money gaming in your midst." God should be the focus of your worship as He refreshed their memories of their forefathers. Profound statements were given as He quoted, word by word, line by line, paragraph by paragraph from texts of old, that they all knew. The entrance area became clear as He spoke to the money exchangers and a multitude of people. They all asked him questions of his authority and he gave them answers they thought God only knew. From this event His name, teachings, and truths became more popular as the local government became more bitter. He continued to travel, teach his closest companions and explained, **"why He was born," "what He has to do," and "where He is going."**

On more of his travels He spoke about eternal existence. This place (an actual location) He describes has endless existence tortures, of the mind, body and spirit. Here at eternal existence there is ultimate pain and suffering that man has never known, but exists. The law of the land there are none. No food, no drink, no shelter, no clothing, or housing. The body (united) with the mind and spirit intact will have their senses, working. The eyes will be able to see hot fiery flames. The body decaying in rot, burns, with their body parts not functioning. The body will be able to feel the skin burning, swelling, pimples forming and bursting, rashes, and wrinkles. The body movements will be limited to confined quarters of inchly movements. Cut, cut, scrape, scrape, burn, burn, decay, decay, rot, rot, will be the confined torments of bodily inchly movements. With this confinement setting, the hunger, thirst for drink will not be satisfied, as there are none available.

The conversations will be heard only to the one speaking, as there will be "no" communication to another. Talk, talk as the lips burn; talk, talk as the skin, tongue, face, receives high scorching temperatures of burning heat while you're in total darkness. This is a mystery to understand and to believe or not believe. There are millions of mysteries here on planet earth. At eternal existence being in the dark and tormented by extremely high temperatures of burning heat is another mystery not fully understood but exists. Those who dwell at eternal existence, the "why" they are there is understood by them.

Once captured in eternal existence your mind will be able to think but none of your thoughts can be shared to others. The mind will be able to think of times past, present happenings and future thoughts. This individual communication will occur at all moments to only thyself, without stops, as there are no clocks or time outs.

During a boat voyage out on the deep waters with His closest followers, the weather elements took a turn for the worst. The sea waters created high waves that lifted the boat to and fro, almost capsizing the crew into the waters. The winds blew at such high speeds moving the waters into the boat rapidly. The boat and crew slowly sinking into the deep sea where in times past took on the dead. The crew members called out to their leader as he woke from sleep. "Master!" they called as He received a new name. With His voice He spoke to the weather elements: "**Be still,**" and all was calm. The Master got out of the boat, walked on the water as His crew members watched with amazement. Even the weather elements obeyed him! "Greater are those who believe who have not seen this occurrence, than those who had to see in order to believe." He then walked on the calm sea waters as one of His closest followers did the same. As He spoke of "His" and their only purpose in this life is to believe, whence I came, why I am here. The mission is rapidly unfolding, to see, feel, hear and receive this eternal life with God.

The "Master" of the weather elements and the universe, as He received this new name, began to talk about His truths and the narrow pathway to the eternal kingdom of God. The boat finally made it to the shore where there was a multitude of people gathered.

A great multitude of people gathered on the seashore to hear the words of truth and His ability to quote passages, verses from texts of old with explanations. Many of the people knew these writings and understood the message. The "Master" taught about forgiveness. The purpose of why I came into this world is to forgive those of their trespasses against the holy, eternal spirit of God of heaven. When I go, and I will soon, I will go and prepare a place for those who believe in Me and whence I came. For it is written, "In my father's house there are many mansions." **All authority of power has been given to Me to prepare a new kingdom of eternal life with the holy eternal, holy spirit God**.

Forgiveness starts with Me to forgive you of your trespasses. To forgive others for their wrongs is the reason "why" I was born. From the beginning of time (the exact date unknown) to today's date, all these wrongs are directed to and against the holy, eternal, spirit God.

He became more popular from His speeches and His miracles performed. The crowds gathered to listen, to watch intensely this man who claims to be God. Questions were asked to him about life, death, the beginning, the end, eternal life and eternal existence. He shouts to the crowd, "**I have the power**

over death. Death where is thy sting, for those who believe in Me." A few listening were inquisitive about death since their beloved brother just died. Their brother was placed in a grave, dead. "Death, where is thy sting if you believe in Me?" Come, Master, I believe you! Have my brother receive your gift of eternal life. Please depart to your brother, he was dead and now alive. Many heard this dialogue between the women and the Master about her brother who died, yet many still did not believe He has the power over death. The women went her way only to find her brother alive. This woman proclaimed the Master's name and this event throughout the land. The Master left the multitude of people with a few of his closest followers to begin to instruct them.

I am He who came into this world so you may have (present tense) life and have it more abundantly.

The warnings! I must first alert you to **eternal existence**, whereupon one's death there is wailing and gnashing of teeth without end. The hot fiery flames, the darkness, and the body torments have been prepared for all those evil spirits first; second, to those who do not believe in Me.

Who am I? If one asks, "**I am that I am.**" Why am I here? So I will receive the sin curse of the evil spirit. Where am I going? I am traveling to teach, instruct others to do the same, that the gift of eternal life now exists, for the taking, by you just doing the asking. How long will it take? Shortly I will say, "It is finished." This brief instruction from the Master left many of His closest followers puzzled.

The Master informed them, "You have been chosen by the holy, eternal, spirit God to be with Me! Go and inform all the gift of eternal life with God is now at hand." His closest followers departed with the spirit gift of the Master to show others His evidence of truth.

The Master of truths traveled to the next town, as most towns and villages were close in distance. His total miles traveled in His lifetime was one hundred miles (only estimating). He traveled by boat, animals, but mostly on foot. Each time upon stopping to speak many gathered to listen. Toward the end of His speeches He would answer questions with demonstrated evidence that **He was God, the Chosen One**.

He talked about the sicknesses of the body and why they will occur to all. The body was created to die, return to the earth from whence it came. During the life of the body it will incur sicknesses, decay because of its short life span (approximately three score plus ten years). This happening (body decay, sicknesses) occurred in the beginning of the human race and occurs still to this present day of history.

"My world," proclaims the Master, is not here in, rather here after, where there are no sicknesses, death or unruly spirits. Sicknesses sometimes will be healed without blemish, upon the will of the holy, eternal God to show His evidence of truth and mercy. He spoke for hours to a multitude of followers about diseases, sickness, death, and to believe in Him than any other known gods of that day. People were doubting His words and belief in Him because some have heard these stories before by others who claim the same. These others practice witchcraft, bribery and trickery to the town folk who all failed. A women spoke with a loud voice to the Master, "I believe in you. My son is full of leprosy (a disease of the skin, muscles with bursting pimples and rashes covering the entire body) since birth." The Master spoke, "Bring your son to Me." As the Master prayed, He touched the unclean man full of leprosy and instantly he became clean, pure and disease-free. The multitude of observers watched the evidence of this miracle that only God could do; they left quickly to tell many what just took place. The man, who was full of leprosy, now cleansed pure without blemish, departed the scene to spread this good news, "**<u>God is with us</u>**." Some doubting people saw to believe, others had to touch the man to believe, many believed who had not seen, yet many left not believing. Greater are those who did not see to believe than those who saw in order to believe.

The Master continued His journey through the region preaching about eternal existence. Most of his teachings were to warn people about this eternal judgment (the word eternal from this writing means forever) and (the word judgment from this writing means penalty). This eternal judgment means total separations from "Him," the holy, eternal, spirit, God.

This place of eternal existence has (past tense) already been prepared for all those one-third evil angelic spirits that dwelt with Me. Prior to the creation of the earth with everything that is found within and without, this horrific place of torture known as eternal existence was then created. This place of eternal existence is for all those spirits who have no believe in Me, why I came into this world. Fire, brimstone, burnings, the skin peeling, the eyes wrinkle, the mouth thirsting for water, the body moving inchly, feeling bitter, angry thoughts, mad, depressant, conversations with no reply, inhaling smoke, coughing, stomach hunger, extreme high temperatures, being enclosed, no sleep, no rest, no day, no night, no food, no friends, no walking, the mind, body and spirit being tormented, of which cannot be fully described from an earthly perspective.

This place, eternal existence, is prepared for all those one-third evil angelic spirits that were removed from their spiritual residence for rebelling against their creator, the holy, eternal spirit God and for those spirits who have no belief in Me.

My truths are explained: with God you need to believe, with God you can have everything, with God all things are possible, with God you have victory, with God you have eternal life, with God the evil spirits don't have you, with God you will not be thrown into the lake of fire, with God all things are done for you, with God there is a mansion being prepared for you (that has been in the making for approximately two thousand years, earth time), with God you will receive a new body, with God you'll reap more abundantly here on earth and at eternal life, with God you'll know Him personally now and for all eternity, with God, God will, has, is, working for you always.

Without God, you will be with the one-third evil angelic spirits, and those rebelling earthly spirits upon your death in eternal existence; without God, you will receive the wrath of God for all eternity; without God, you will not receive the gift of eternal life; without God, you cannot breathe, talk, move, think, learn, eat or do anything. You are a created spiritual being for God's honor and glory. To rebel against a holy, eternal, spirit God will, upon your death, be captured in **eternal existence**.

The huge crowd heard these teachings and were amazed how a person dressed like a shepherd gave evidence he was God. A person with doubt spoke up and told a story to the Master about her child who was born blind. Years have passed, now he's a young man, still blind. Master, I believe you are God. Come cure my son's blindness. With His compassion, the young man was brought forth through the crowd to the Master. The Master prayed, touched the man and his blindness was no more. The crowd continued following the Master as His popularity increased. The rulers, governors and those in charge of government saw and heard these miracles and became bitter. For it is written, "God will come and the government will be on His shoulders," claiming He is, or is equal to, God.

During this time of history (two thousand years ago, approximately), their were many who claimed to be God. It has been written, "**There's nothing new under the sun**." Today at this time of history there are those who claim to be God or will be a God some day. This Master wrote, etched in stone,

"Have no other gods besides Me, I'm a jealous God." One needs to ponder which god or gods are the right answer. Let's look at the evidence an eyewitness described.

As he traveled throughout the lands, He would always stop to talk to the crowds that were following Him or took the time to talk to individuals with needs. On one occasion He was walking alone and came to a fountain of well water. There was a woman beside herself trying to fill a pail of water. No one was there to help her, when suddenly the Master spoke to the woman. Surprised and shocked, she turned toward the Master. This woman did not know of His popularity or the miracles he had done. The woman looked discretely at the man, recognizing that her people were not in favor of His people as fighting took place among the two. He and she were the only ones present at this gathering. When the Master asked her for water, she replied, "Don't you know that between us there should be no conversation because our people have claims against the other?"

The Master spoke with wisdom and understanding, and told her everything about the history of her life that she thought was in secret, giving her details of her life of what she was doing yesterday. She was in *shock* when he told her she had five husbands!

Today you are gathering water to drink. I am here to offer you living water where you will thirst no more. The woman was much surprised how this stranger knew her history of wrongful doings even up to the day they were speaking. She spoke to him saying, "Don't you know that we are enemies between us?" The Master said, "I have come for all, that all may not perish, to believe in my truths, that **I am the way, the truth, the eternal life**. Believe in Me, whence I came, why I'm here for your eternal life." She marveled, left to tell all she met a man who told her everything she ever did and claiming He was God!

Your will will decide your fate. Your will decides for you right or wrong. Your will will try to be captured by the evil, demonic spirits. Your will will govern your thoughts, words, and deeds. Your will will explain why you rebel against the holy, eternal spirit God. Your will will be introduced to the way of eternal life. Your will will receive judgment on Judgment Day. Your will will be tempted by trickery, quackery, lust, adultery, fornication, uncleanness, lasciviciousness, idolatry, witchcraft, hatred, variance, emulations, wrath, strife, seditions, heresies, envy, murders, drunkenness, revellings and others. Your will will try to be captured by the evil, demonic spirits to have you enter eternal existence, or your will will enter eternal life with the Creator of all things by a holy, eternal, spirit God. Your will, will?

CHAPTER FIVE

<u>EVOLUTION OF MAN</u>

The evolution of man has no beginning, end, or any explanation why the human race exists. Through evolution, man has created this thought process of how everything came into existence. From the creepy crawler, the hairy two-legged animals, to a look-alike man, evolutionists believe, "Now comes the human race!" This thought takes an extreme amount of faith to believe! Textbooks have been written to explain this, colleges and universities of courses of instruction which teach the same, cultures pass this thought process down the culture chain, all of which that evolution is how the human race began.

This evolution of man makes no mention of God. This is a good example of man's ways vs. God's way. Simply stated, "God has been left out of this thought process." Now it is up to man to explain everything. Did the creepy crawler create man or did it happen in reverse, or did it never happen at all. Your will will believe or not believe.

The evolution of man has no dates, times, places of origin, where you're going, where you've been, just a belief system that has no correct answers. The evidence can be found in written texts of old day to prove evolution is not happening or it did not ever happen. These texts from old day (perhaps some of the oldest and most preserved texts of all time) state: Animals are to multiply after their own kind. Creepy crawler animals multiply after creepy crawler animals. Two-legged hairy animals multiply after two-legged animals, and so with birds, fish, and the human race. From day one till this present day all animals multiply after their own kind. Evolution is still only a thought process by man.

The Big Bang theory of man's origin is a prior occurrence, then evolution. This theory is just an educated guess of the human race's beginning and that is why it's called the Big Bang theory, not the Big Bang fact. You can learn a lot about the title of something if you define the words describing the event. Many well known, highly educated people believe in this theory of how this world (Planet Earth) was formed.

The first question that should be asked is, "What fueled the spark to create the Bang?" Sounds reasonable! Second question: "Who was around during that time of history to hear the Big Bang? When did this Big Bang begin? Who is the original author stating this occurrence occurred? How long did it take from the day of the Big Bang to what is known of today?

Questions, questions and more questions need to be asked with correct answers to be provided, if any belief in any origin of the human race is to be believed.

CHAPTER SIX

RELIGIONS AND MAN

Everywhere on Planet Earth there are religions. To belong to most of these religions you have to do something or be someone with works to do. You might say, "These are working religions in order to belong." Trying to work within some religions to gain respect of the members is an accomplishment that many are doing. Work, work, be good, be good, take a test and achieve the next level of accomplishment is a practice of many religions. Some of these religions have you dress up in your finest attire in order to attend. During worship you'll see others in charge dress in such fine linen that you would not see them elsewhere in this clothing. The bright colors of clothing, jewels they're wearing, spotted paint makeup on their faces and body, chanting sounds with no interpretations, are everyday common practices of some religions. It's alright to belong as long as you don't ask why things are happening the way they are.

Having tools in their hands while hitting objects (of unknown value), steam in the air without definition, muttering words of no meaning, describes a religion commonly known to man and is found on all continents. Within the buildings of worship you'll find numerous statues of people (some with no names) glaring out at you as you gaze at the statue. Most of these statues are of people who are dead and were created into material images without the use of pictures. What you're looking at is just a statue image of what this person might have resembled. The statues are mostly male in origin but there is at least one woman. The statue materials are of great wealth such as gold, silver, bronze, diamonds and other precious metals. It has been said that some of these statutes, when properly addressed, can forever forgive your wrongs against the holy, spirit, eternal God. The man who claims to be God states, "It is wrong to have any other God besides Me. **I have come into this world so that through Me and Me alone you can be saved from eternal existence and enter eternal life where I reside.**"

Other religions of the Far East of old days and to this very day offer bloody sacrifices to their gods. Their gods are mostly made from precious metals molded into images to be worshipped. What's common to most of these material gods is a hot fiery flame burning within the statue. The statue sizes of these gods all vary from god to god, some rather huge in shape and others quite small. Within the statue the bloody sacrifice takes place. There's a lot of chanting, music and dancing while the sacrifice is being offered, until the fire goes out, then the sacrifice is over. It's not known how many daily, weekly or monthly sacrifices there are or why, who, where, when or how each sacrifice is done, just that some are done. Written information is not found with exact details about this kind of worship.

God's within some religions; if you belong, you'll be a god, too! This religion takes on membership. This membership of this religion boasts of thousands, possibly millions, found worldwide. A religion that rewrote the text of old day to promote their own religion their way – wow! Did this happen? Yes! For it is written from texts of "old," do not write, change or alter the collective books by this supreme author as the plagues that are found within will come upon you! **Such a warning**!

This religion of great material wealth explains a process of how you can become a god or equivalent to one. The leaders in charge of its membership are quite clever in the role they plan. The questions asked of them mostly go unanswered as most of its membership doesn't ask questions of why they're doing what they're doing. The songs they sing, the instruments they play, the music is delightful to hear but from their origin this religion is out of tune with the one, true, holy, eternal, spirit God.

To choose a religion or not to choose a religion, that is the question! Could a religion choose you? How many religions are there (possibly in excess of thousands)? Religions with God or without God, do they exist? Yes! Travel a bit, talk to some, read about religions and you'll find many questions go unanswered.

New religions are on the horizon! These new religions find their way to all of the seven continents. Many devoted worshippers are found within these religions. Who created some of these religions? (Answer most unknown.) But what is known, they exist.

On a continent where the equator is beaming its heat are found numerous tribal religions. Some of these tribal religions have no textbooks, no buildings, no known God, no revenues, no set of rituals, no leaders in charge. What is found mostly is just chanting (without interruption), dancing and music. The languages spoken are unclear to their meaning. Nearby another tribe has their own religion quite opposite of their direct neighbors. Of the many languages found within this land area on Planet Earth there's more than one hundred different languages spoken. Most of the religions here are tribal in nature and possibly might have begun on day one.

The facts are that today many tribal religions do exist without texts, clarity or a purpose for existing. You need to examine all the evidence, eyewitnesses, valid truths, future predictions, and current happenings before choosing a religion or a belief in a holy, eternal, spirit, God. It is written, "Seek and you'll find. Knock and the door will be open. Ask and thou shall receive." These once spoken, now written, words have been recorded in history for thousands of years. **It is yours for the taking for you just by asking**.

Most religions have one thing in common with the other. The members or worshippers of these religions, in order to belong, have to do something, give something, be something, worship something, acquire something, attend something, buy something, or numerous other somethings. There's is only "one" from old day to this day that states from the first written text in the English language, "I'll accept you just as you are!" There are no somethings to do. "I've done it all for you." These words were written down from one of the oldest texts known. This text has been written down first with ink (by hand) more times than any text in recorded history. With today's technology of print and communications, this text is the number one printed, copied and distributed than any other book known. You might say, "God has revealed Himself to the human race without error."

From all of the religions, God's here on Planet Earth to choose one man who claims to be the one-true-holy-spirit-God who will offer Himself to you. Your will, will choose this path toward Him or your will, will not. You can now say your will has a purpose in your life. This purpose is **why you were born**! The greatest decision in your life is to decide on accepting the gift of eternal life that "today' is being offered to you freely without any "somethings" to do. The spiritual war that exists within your life has been won and it is yours to receive.

Look around where you live on Planet Earth. From a scientific glance, is the human race properly inhabiting the earth? Let's look at some facts. Past wars, present wars and more wars to come as it has been foretold from texts of old. The longest war (time-wise) is between the one, true, holy, eternal, spirit, God and the most beautiful, most intelligent created spirit who from his "free will" turned evil, demonic, with hatred toward his Creator. **That's a fact**! This spiritual war has been going on long before you were born, before there was time or space, before you could accept His free gift of eternal life! Wow! Now you know there is a spiritual war in progress. Both want your eternal spirit for eternity. What are you going to do? What are you going to do? What are you going to do? When the created evil, demonic spirit comes for you?

This spiritual war is known only to a few, it has a beginning (whence it began) and a dramatic, sinful, painful, tortured end (in eternal existence). It's not over till it's over! The written information about this spiritual war is found (in precise details) and has been distributed to all nations so all can know. This book, of these dramatic details about the war, is found from the number one written book of all time.

The other wars that are documented from history are between: man vs. man, government vs. government, country vs. country, state vs. state, nation vs. nation, tribe vs. tribe, religion vs. religion, and many other combinations in between. These wars were foretold prior to their happenings and the last war here on Planet Earth will devastate Planet Earth. There will be no more yelling or shouting, it will be over! War and wars have been around ever since the human race began occupation of Planet Earth. The family wars (of all types) happen and are happening till this very day. The wisest man who ever lived said: "There's nothing new under the sun." This saying and quote is heard often by people and its origin came from He. This man was a king of his people because of his truthful knowledge that was given Him by His God, who is the one, true, holy, eternal, spirit God. As he sat upon His throne, people came before Him for law and justice. The amazement of the people were astonish on each truthful decision that came forth by Him. One notable trial came forth when two women brought a child before the king's court, both claiming birth rights of the child. This king said, "Cut the child in half, give half to the other." "No!" declared the women. The king's judgment entered, "Give the child to the mother who spoke up; she's the mother."

Wars of man continued to occur during this time of history and is still occurring in today's date. Hundreds? No! Thousands? No! Millions? No! Billions? Yes! Billions of people have died from the known wars of Planet Earth. "Once you die then the judgment." This occurs one per person. The earthly body enters the earth whence it came, then the eternal spirit is judged.

The population of the human race here on Planet Earth during the year 2007 is approximately six billion people. This number equals the amount of people who have died from fighting in these wars. Wars, wars and more wars will come, so one can only ponder the total number of deaths from the human race will be. Man's righteousness upon himself so far equals one death per person as of the year 2007. Is man's righteousness good? No! **"There is no one that is good," declares the man who claims to be God.**

CHAPTER SEVEN

<u>HEAVEN AND EARTH</u>

Man has described many known facts about Planet Earth, yet many facts are still unknown. To name some of these are: oceans, land masses, clouds, animals, planets, and more, yet there are more unknown. The waters, land areas, and even the many varieties of animals are being discovered with little or no information about these discoveries. Formulas for gases, air quality, and energy of all types are coming to the fore light of the human race but all have been around since earth's origin. From the advent of the computer, the "pin size" computer chips, the communication age is rapidly present during the year 2007. More important than this information of communication is this: the most common question asked of all people, **"Why am I here?"** This means you! What purpose do I have while I'm living? The questions will be answered as you read along. First an explanation is needed to know about Planet Earth.

Man, with his ability to think, reason, dream like no other living creature, has created his way on how Planet Earth came into existence. This information is written down in numerous books. Some of these ways of earth's creation by man are: stars falling (question should be falling from where?), explosions occurred when earth was created (Who lit the fuse?), Big Bang theory of earth's creation (Who heard the bang? How loud was it?), planets' gods created the earth (Who created these planet gods? Says who?), solar gods (Will the energy run out?), another universe gods (How many are there? Who's number one or in charge of the other? Need evidence here!). There are more gods than these and more gods to come!

Each god mentioned or way of earth's creation needs a belief system to believe or not to believe— that one, all, or none of these earth's creations are correct. You must remember that the human race was not around to see, feel, touch or hear these events happening. Man's free will can decide to believe or not to believe. That is the question? You may have a belief of how the world came into existence.

Planet Earth has what no other planet has and that is it contains life and eternal spirits. (Life by this description implies that all life living will die) and (eternal spirits like the human race will reside forever, just depending upon where: eternal life or eternal existence). All other planets, stars, universes, galaxies, solar systems have one thing in common: there's no life on board! The complexities of the earth are so complex the mind of man cannot fully understand its nature. Looking around at the earth's systems and components, one needs to ponder on how or why everything was put together and even why you, yes you! are involved in this process. History records the human race of being on Planet Earth for only a few thousand years. The exact time or dates are not known and are not important, just that man did have his beginning on Planet Earth a few thousands years ago.

The free will of man is the same today as back then of his origin. (Now you can say: some things do stay the same.) Earth's population of humanity as of 2007 is approximately six billion people. The exact number of people is unknown because many third world countries do not keep records. Going back in time of just a hundred years the population of earth would be less. Right? The population of the human race from recorded history would be less as each century passes. This would continue to occur from A.D. to B.C. Given this knowledge of common sense of the earth's population would decrease in history. A belief of today could be: In the beginning there was only a man and a woman who began earth's residence. (One of the oldest and most well preserved texts indicates this happening.) The earth at that time of only two occupants represents the purest of nature as it was intended to be. The land areas, bodies of water, the views of the universe, animals and having a direct, personal relationship of the eternal, holy, spirit, God was happening on day one of earth's creation and is happening today of those exercising their "free will" to their Creator.

Early man (on day one) traveled around mostly on foot discovering the beauty of the earth and not knowing why or how things came to being. His travels (only estimating) could possibly be a few hundred miles. The location of his living quarters is important, as if he arrived in time and space near the ice, the human race would have failed. The location of early man began near the equator suited his needs best. Man observed the earth from the beginning and saw much of what is still known today; most continents have sand on the seashore, salt found in ocean waters, trees of all types, animals too many to count and name, wind that blows, the sun shines for light, the moons that give lesser light, twenty-four hours per day, seven days per week, twelve months per year, three hundred sixty-five days a year. Yes! You could say history has a way of repeating itself.

Man needs to determine why he exists and the purpose of life. **Man is a spirit creation, like all spirits will last forever**. This is true today like it was in the beginning. Spirits will last forever in eternal life or will be captured in eternal existence. God spoke with nobody present, spirit angels spoke to man, evil demonic spirits spoke from within the human body—are those happenings true? Written evidence, personal testimony and eyewitnesses confirm these are.

So, **why you exist is quite simple**, to determine which road you'll choose. The wide road traveled by most will lead to <u>eternal existence</u> when your last breath is exhaled. The narrow road will lead you to <u>eternal life</u> where your holy, eternal, spirit God awaits you. Which road is better for you? Your only eternal purpose in life is to have you choose which road to go down. You can now say you have been given the knowledge of "**why**" you exist. This is to choose from your (free will) the narrow road (because many will be called to go, like you, but most will decline the gift) of eternal life. Truth will guide you through till you've reached the end of earth's life. Choosing the broad road there is no end!

The eternal existence broad road of life could start out great, such as: wealth, work, travel, fame, fortune, good looks, popularity, business success, earthly mansions, vacations, servants, specialty foods to eat, dining pleasures, sexual pleasures, winning, and then... death occurs. You're captured in eternal existence. At this place (an actual setting) without time, limited space (no place to roam), and now the wrath of the eternal, holy, spirit God is prevailing. What did you earn? Why are you here and others not? Your earthly possessions and the Planet Earth god took control over you during your short life (three score plus ten years) for now what purpose? You're now alone, will be alone, forever torture of the mind, body and eternal spirit alone!

The narrow road (how narrow) so narrow vs. the broad road that many are called to follow (like you) but more chose not to travel. This is now your choice to be chosen by the Creator, holy, spirit, eternal God of all things material and spiritual to go the narrow pathway of eternal life. Today your "free will" can choose this path as tomorrow this choice may not be available. The narrow road is rough, bumpy, rocky with many obstacles to overcome. Accepting this free gift of eternal life and traveling down this road the number one obstacle that will be against you is from this god of Planet Earth. The most intelligent (smarter than any human), beautiful (beyond description to describe), created spirit (which will live everlasting in eternal existence) is the devil which will tempt you daily to do wrong. This devil (singular) and his "hosts" of demonic spirits will sidetrack you, confuse you, tease you, taunt you, enter sins in your life... but upon your death you will (not maybe) or (hopefully) not be captured in eternal existence where the skin burns and the body barely turns.

Eternal life starts here on Planet Earth immediately upon accepting this free gift from the holy, eternal, spirit God of heaven where he resides. When your last breath is exhaled on Planet Earth and the body stops functioning, the first breath of eternal life is inhaled forever in heaven. At this blink of an eye of time and space, your Creator, "a man who claims to be God," will greet you upon heaven's entrance. One person he'll greet at a time, one by one will enter these pearly gates until the entrance will be closed with no further comings or goings. At this moment this will be your gift (yourself) to give to your Creator by accepting his free gift of eternal life.

Heaven can wait! Many have said, but never finished their sentence, Wait for what? Much is not known about heaven compared to eternal existence. The most important things have been written and recorded about heaven from an earthly perspective that's enough. Paradise living, mansions built by their

Creator one mansion per person, delightful settings, ultimate glory and praises to the holy, eternal, spirit God, revealing truths, minus: pains, wrongs, evil spirits, liars, deaths, darkness, sleep, suffering, tortures, corruptions, no food, no drink, no life and all unrighteousness.

Heaven plus: a new body (same spirit), a new name (one name per person), light 24/7, no time, no sleep, no worries! Mansions, dwellings, traveling the universe (faster than the speed of light), give praises to the holy, eternal, spirit God; a new heaven (currently under construction), and a new earth (currently being put together) is being created for all those human spirits of Planet Earth who (only one requirement) accept this free gift from this man – who? – claims to be God! Two thousand earth years in the making as this new earth and heaven when complete will host the servants for the holy, eternal, spirit God. Conversations with your Creator, other human spirits by their (new name), conversations with angelic spirits with no bodies which all have names (one per spirit) and receiving all knowledge about everything awaits this happening. You'll remember everything; no schools, textbooks or tests, "Ask and thou shall receive."

One of the oldest known books records the earth was created in six twenty-four hour days. The intelligence gathering of such an accomplishment is beyond comprehension to understand fully. Now you need to have a vision of a new heaven and a new earth that is taking more than two thousand earth years to create from the same Creator who put the earth

together in just six days. Wow! This is on the horizon
for those who believe this to be true. This happening
is an example of God's glory and promises that he
cannot share with anyone. Currently in heaven there
is no time. This new earth and heaven is just a voice
command away from happening.

The new heaven and earth will be created for those
(human beings only) who have received the gift of
eternal life from God. This gift can only be accepted
while you're living. This gift is giving your wrongs,
trespasses, and sins to this man who claims to be God
and in return you'll receive (not maybe) eternal life.
Your earthly wrongs will be forgotten. Your sins will
vanish as far as the east is from the west. They will be
remembered no more! Upon heaven's entrance (only
one way) all memories of old Planet Earth, the seven
continents, oceans, governments, wars, famines, and
unsaved people will be remembered no more. Think!
If remembrance did occur in the new heaven, there
would lie sins. **So sins and heaven don't mix.** Planet
Earth, today's way of living, "will soon be over." No
way? Yes! God's way.

What is faster than the speed of light? What is
faster than a blink of your eyes/ Able to walk through
walls! Travel without energy! Only those saved earthly
human spirits who have entered heaven immediately
upon their earthly death will accomplish this. All
former things (whatever they might be) have passed
way. "Behold all things have become new." "New"
will have a new definition; simply stated, "new" will
mean all things: material and spiritual will last for
eternity. The holy, eternal, spirit God will speak His

words, and this new heaven and earth will come into existence for His honor, glory and His ways. This occurrence will be faster than a blink of an eye and all things prophesied now come to existence. This was all done with "**hope**" – **you'll be there**.

CHAPTER EIGHT

<u>GOD KNOWS YOU</u>

The created eternal, existence, spirit, earth god knows you. This god knows all people, all spirits in times past to this very day of history. Most people do not know this god exists or for what purpose this god was created. The most intelligence, quick wit, beautiful, charming, convincing spirit earth god has a host (the amount not known, not important) of evil spirits to assist in all his wrongdoings that leads others (human beings only) to believe they're good. **He wants you, he wants you, he wants you as a new recruit** and will do anything to achieve this! This earth spirit god knows people love darkness vs. light. Darkness by this definition is: satisfying yourself to have and do what this world has to offer. This darkness could be wealth, looks, job, business, lust, sports, recreation and any and all things that keep you from the narrow road that brings you to eternal life.

The purpose of this eternal existence earth god is to create wrong things in your life in which you think are right. Second purpose is to have right things that do exist and have you think they're wrong. As of the year 2007, this master craftsman and most intelligent created spirit god has been practicing the "art" of this craft for two thousand years toward the human race only. Many (human beings only) have been, are, and will be captured in eternal existence by this evil, demonic, satanic earth god. This earth god will **work on you, work on you, work on you** your entire life until he wins or fails. This god, from the very early years of your life till your old age 24/7, till your last breath, this earth god's purpose is to capture as many of the human race spirits in and at eternal existence. The two thousand years of practice, wit, charm, giving, desires and planning means that this "art" of deceiving brings you on the broad road of life that transforms you into eternal existence upon your death if you don't ask for the gift of eternal life. Remembering, "Ask and thou shall receive." Receive what? Eternal life! From whom? A man who claims to be God! Why? The purpose of why He was born to honor and glorify the eternal, holy, spirit, God.

Material things, material things and more material things this earthly god will give you. It's OK to have things as long as those material things don't have you. For it is written, "What would it profit a man if he gain and receive the whole world," but lost his spirit in eternal existence?

This earth god is a spirit. A spirit you cannot see, touch, feel or hear. This is common for all spirits that do not have a body. When an evil spirit or spirits enter a human body, most times it takes over a portion or all of the body functions. The person who is "possessed" has lost control of his mind and body while the evil, demonic, spirit is within. At this time all wrongs will take place: stealing, killing, anger, lust, and crimes of all kinds. During these happenings witnesses are observing these actions taking place. This Planet Earth god is building a "kingdom" of evil spirits for his final destiny at eternal existence which is a "**copycat**" of his creator, "building his kingdom of spirits with bodies at eternal life." So this created spirit creature known as the god of Planet Earth wants you to fall within his traps of his confined spaces at eternal existence, where all rebelling angelic and human spirits will be forever.

This earthly god will finally be captured and resume in a place especially prepared for him before the foundation of the world was created. This happening has been foretold with words and now it's in written form for those to believe or not to believe.

When human wars break out most times the end result is unknown. From recorded history man's wars against man the end result nobody wins because shortly thereafter another war begins. This spiritual war has a beginning, is currently occurring, you are part of it, and the ending is known to be: **eternal existence or eternal life, your will? Will?**

The eternal God of eternal life who resides in heaven, Creator of all things material and spiritual, knows you, knows your thoughts, words you speak, your deeds and everything you do before they occur.

Before you think, walk, talk, run, breathe, sleep, enjoy, grieve, this God, which is the only one, true God, knows your everything. Why? or how? Good question! Because it is written, "All things that were created were created by Him, for Him, for His honor and glory." This God knows of other said gods as he said, "Have no other gods before Me, as I am a jealous God." The air you breathe, the ground you walk, what you see, the food you eat, the things you touch, and everything that exists, it's not yours! This holy, eternal, spirit God is very patient but when your last breath is exhaled then the judgment of your eternal spirit awaits.

This God of eternal heaven explains how this earth was created with all of its complexities, systems, components and spiritual life. When this God spoke, "everything came into existence." **Wow**! **From the sound of His voice all things were put together**.

The eternal life, spirit God who (**self-sustains Himself**) knows you from times past, all present happenings and your entire future. A known fact about you is: your voice, body style, talents, looks, charm, age and other types are totally different from any other person. Yes! You're one of a kind! Yes! You were created by this God. This God is working for you. His working demonstrates to all, the evidence and the nature of God. God knows you before you were born, knows your every thought before you think, knows when you're going to speak and what you spoke before you spoke. This God knows the beginning and ending of your life and if your free will will accept his gift of eternal life!

The nature of the human race is very complex. This complexity is evidence of God's work, of the billions of people born (only estimating) two are not alike. The voice is not the same, skin color is different, tall, short, fast, slow, talents not the same, different fingerprints, DNA all different, yet many common traits are found.

Common traits among people are: free will, living eternal spirit, came into the world the usual way, will live, will die, will eat, will sleep, will be captured by the evil, demonic, earth god in eternal existence or accept the gift of eternal life (only while you're alive) and enter eternal life.

The holy, eternal, spirit God wants you to decide: light vs. darkness, right vs. wrong, living in eternal existence or living in eternal life. I'm your God vs. I'm not your God. New body, new name vs. old decaying body, same name. My ways vs. demonic, satanic ways. Life vs. death. Travel the universe vs. no body movements. Peace, tranquility, meekness vs. anger, bitterness, skin burning, torture, heat. Receive the created, earthly existence god vs. receiving the one, true, holy, eternal, spirit God. **Your will? will?**

God knows you and everything else. The time you wake up, your daily activities, sleep time, your house, furniture, auto and all your internal organs. It has been said, "that you were thought of before the world was created," then you were created at this time and placed here on Planet Earth. You are part of God's eternal life plan. This plan works and you need to be a partaker, yours just for the asking!

Remembering this is God's plan to have you accept him. "<u>**Now is the accepted time**</u>," today.

CHAPTER NINE

<u>SPIRITS</u>

S pirits are eternal beings created by one, true, holy
God, eternal spirit. **Spirits, both human and
angelic, will last forever**. Forever is a long time. Both
of these spirits have the same nature. Their destinies
will reside forever at a place especially prepared for
them before there was time and space. This prepara-
tion space is **<u>eternal life or eternal existence</u>**, which
are separated from one another by a huge gulf. In
eternal existence (those who dwell there) know who's
in eternal life. The eternal life (recipients) of this free
eternal gift, from this man "who claims to be God"
do not know who dwells at eternal existence. Sounds
fair? Sounds reasonable? Remembering! God's ways
vs. man's ways will prevail.

In the beginning (the exact date unknown) there
were more angelic spirits than human being spirits.
These angelic spirits have no bodies. All spirits have
a free will, can choose right or wrong, just like you

can do. A free will can choose the way of truth or the way of lawlessness. Which is better? Well, consider laws. All laws created by man from all lands and dates of time have been, currently are being broken. Thousands of laws there are about guns. All have been broken. One text of "old day" states, "**Thou shall not kill**," pondering, what more do you need!

Spirits from an earthly eye you cannot see. The wind you cannot see but realize there is wind. So is an angelic spirit like the wind, travels fast and whence it came it's not known. Human spirits are temporarily placed within the body till the body dies. At this time of human death the spirit leaves the body to enter eternal life or eternal existence. The commonality among all spirits is free will, communication, travel to and fro, able to speak to an eternal God, work, rest, give praise, give anger, knows right, knows wrong, eternal life and eternal existence are known, gives and takes commands, knows other spirits, knows human spirits, angelic spirits cannot multiply after their own kind, will always be a spirit, spirits don't eat, sleep, thirst and have limited energy provided by a holy, eternal, spirit God.

Spirits are a mystery to us, as you need to have faith to believe there are spirits or faith there are no spirits. Conversations from the holy, eternal, spirit God to fellow man has been on record numerous times from old ancient writings. The holy God spoke to man, man spoke back. God could see man, man could not see God. At this time a conversation took place revealing God's truths to the human race. These events that took place over hundreds of years must have been an experience worth telling, and written over and over again when fellow man spoke to God, voice to voice. This story during that time in history, up to this present day, is told with much evidence of its happening. These spiritual conversations were written down, copied and recopied more times than any other text so that during this year it is known to us.

Imagine...! You, going through your daily activities at home, work or recreation and suddenly a voice is spoken, calls you by name, is describing what you're doing! This voice is this holy, eternal, spirit God as he introduces himself to you. Unbelievable? Yes! There are eyewitnesses with written evidence to support this. What was the purpose of this God speaking to those in times past? The answer is quite simple. This God wants to have (present tense) a personal relationship with you! Person by person, day by day, year by year, century by century, eternal life by eternal life is God's purpose. **<u>For this is why you were born</u>**.

The only (singular) purpose of your spirit is to have a personal relationship with the one, true, holy, eternal spirit God! For it is written from texts of old day, **"Many are called but few are chosen."** This is occurring today at this time of history. The clock is ticking, your heart is beating, getting older, time is not on your side, tomorrows may not come, with these and other things in your way, the right day is today. During this day and time in history God rarely speaks (verbally) to the human race like in times past. God's direct approach is from his host of spirits, physical and none physical. This God communicates from written texts, eyewitnesses, nature, miracles, <u>a man who claims to be God</u> and from other ways not known to all.

God's written words found in numerous texts have been passed down, preserved more times than any other text. This text, written in more languages than any other text in history. These texts explain who this eternal God is, why you were created by Him, how the world and everything in it was created and the most important part of this book is about you and for you. Excuses, excuses, excuses, no more excuses can be claimed by anyone because they did not know about this holy, eternal, spirit God. This eternal God is very patient and now is the accepted time to ask for His free, eternal gift of salvation (**only entrance requirement to eternal life**).

The world, earth, moons, stars, planets, air, gases, animals, spirits, mountains, human beings, universes, galaxies and more were all created by one, true, holy, eternal God. By "His voice" everything was created by Him, for Him and for you, too!

Of the billions of stars that could possibly exist, the trillions of galaxies that may be and all of the material beauty known to man, created by this holy, eternal, spirit God, they all have this in common: All are made of material substance. They (the material substances) do not have an eternal spirit and have no communication with their Creator. So one could ponder: Hmmm...how boring! The Creator created without sharing any of His glory with anyone. Then a miracle happened! You were thought of before any of these material substances were created. (Now you can say there is a God who thinks.) A material substance was created (name Planet Earth). Then you were born to live an average life (in years) three score plus ten years. Then you'll die. During your earthly life you will be introduced (informally) to this Planet Earth god of beauty, lust, wit, trickery, wealth, evil, all which at all times (24/7) have you avoid the holy, eternal, everlasting, spirit God. Then...the most patient, holy, true, eternal spirit God will proclaim Himself to you. This God will find you where you live, work, play, sleep, commute or anywhere you are. This is God's purpose and your purpose to know Him.

Buildings, buildings, and more buildings have been built and are currently being built to worship this God than any other god in history. Remember! It is written, "Have no other gods besides me. I am a jealous God." In most towns, cities, states, countries, provinces, nations, continents and remote areas there are numerous buildings to enter to worship this eternal, holy, spirit God. Some worship by singing, dancing, listening, lecturing, giving, praising, praying and other ways to worship for their gratitude of entering eternal life with their Creator. For "you" can enter. "Know and you'll receive the gift of eternal life." Here is found life, truth, communication, that: He is the only way, the truth, and is providing His gift of eternal life. **"Yours" for the taking, by "you" just doing the asking**.

God's plan is found from the smallest animal to the largest, and every animal in between, God has a plan for them. Without these animals human life would have difficulty to survive. It has been written, "Man has control over the animals that inhabit the earth." These animals are too many to name and number that fits into the plan of this holy, eternal, spirit God. The purpose of these animals are to distinguish the unique nature of God. When God speaks, people listen and things are created. Yes! God's power is an energy force that self-sustains itself. A force (non-created) that when spoken all actions are performed. God's self-sustaining force always was, always is, and always will be. You "see," "some things do remain the same." The more you learn about this God the more most want to participate because.......... there's a gift waiting for you. This eternal gift is one you don't deserve but today it is offered to you freely. This gift of eternal life is provided for "all" those (human race only) who believe in Him, as the only way to enter eternal life before... **watch out! be careful! en garde!**... before God's trial of the century begins. This eternal existence trial will have no attorneys or jurors, just unsaved human race spirits, demonic angelic spirits and their Creator, this holy, eternal, spirit God.

This trial proclaiming eternal existence judgment against all spirits, "human spirits only," who would not receive his eternal life gift while living here on Planet Earth and for all those demonic angelic spirits who rebelled against Him prior to the creation of mankind. Sounds frightening, scary, lonely, dark, full of torture, miserable, everlasting, **no exits**... well, it is. This trial can be avoided when you accept His gift of eternal life. This trial (will occur) is already marked out on the post calendar and on that trial date will take only earthly seconds to complete, then judgment, eternal sentence to the lake of fire for eternal existence for the body and spirit.

God's plan is all mapped out, forecast; **read all about it**! Pretold by many believers and preachers, clearly written from the #1 distributed text in the world, told to many in person, by a man who claims to be God that this trial will happen (no maybes). The map and text ancient that it is will take place in the Far East. The exact location is unknown.

Today's population is approximately five billion people during the year 2006. Upon these five billion deaths in approximately (three score plus ten) years (pending accepting God's eternal gift), this trial of the century will be massive (people-wise). A few will watch this trial compared to the number of people who will be tried, convicted, and sentenced immediately. The trial will be just, fair and impartial. One by one will stand and come forth without excuses, attorneys or a jury to decide their predetermined fate. The number of people, billions (only estimating) will be tried in a court proceeding that will last only about an earth day long. All people who lived on Planet Earth that rejected to accept the gift of eternal life will be participants at this trial. Together they will hear their charges, will be found guilty, receive their life sentences of eternal existence. This sentence will reveal a place of torture being placed in a burning lake of fire. (**Note: no appeals of sentencing will be heard.**)

At the lake of fire, a description has been fore-told for centuries. This place (physical) there are no comings or goings. The skin burns, rashes develop, pimples burst, with yelling and screaming of all those who dwell there without end. There is no walking, talking to others in conversations, no running or jumping for joy, just being in a tortured state of mind, body and spirit. The confined movement is very little (possibly only inches). The conversation will be only to yourself. The fiery hot flamed tongue will move in extreme pain to speak and no one will hear you!

When you talk your lips move in severe burning pain. When you perspire and thirst there's nothing to drink. Nothing to quench your thirst! Your memory will be quick, sharp and remembering everything of times past (on Planet Earth), how things used to be and post events of eternal existence. Here, time-wise there are no clocks ticking, calendar turning, no spring, winter, summer or fall, no years to count, just pondering in torture. There is no day, no night, no food, no drink, no joy, no happiness, no friends and **no EXITS!** to be found.

This lake of fire (massive in land area) with holding cells of billions and billions was created only for the evil, demonic, angelic spirits who rebel harshly against their Creator. This burning lake (substance unknown), there's hot (possibly hotter than Planet Sun) molten fiery flames from a source that burns continually. This flame cannot be extinguished.

This lake of fire (from an earthy perspective) would be to describe an area of extensive heat much like a volcano. This lake would have volcano lava burning the edges of the body. The lava would retreat for a moment then edge back to the body to burn again. Splashing lava would caress the face of those people who dwell there. The clothing you once had for daily living, none would be found or worn because "all" at eternal existence in this lake of fire are naked. Each body part would be burning slowly, melting without being consumed. This is a mystery (the lake of fire) to completely ponder the final judgment sentence for all those who rebel (humans and angelic spirit angels) against their Creator.

God's plan for you is quite simple. First, you must know the simplicity of God. Keep it plain, keep it simple then you'll understand the nature of this holy, eternal, spirit God. My ways are truth, My ways are for eternal life. This information is found in most libraries worldwide and has not changed from their original writings in thousands of years. God's nature, God's voice, God's writings, God in the flesh, God's worship dwellings, God's universe, God's everything and most important: **God wants you**.

You need to realize that you are a created being, a spirit by nature, and an eternal spirit is all you'll ever be. You're a spirit, God's an eternal, holy spirit as it is written, "Let's make man in our image," so now you know you're an image of this holy, eternal, spirit God.

God over time will work on you, work on you, work on you, to discover that you need this God today, tomorrow (if they should come your way) and forever. How long is forever? (Take time to look up the definition!) What rebels you from God is your earthly nature. (Remembering the one-third angelic spirits who also rebel.) Now knowing their final fate will be placed individually into the lake of fire. You can escape this **wrath of God** by accepting his "free gift" of eternal life.

Your earthly nature, when all added up, are your wrongs that separate you from God. God exists, and only truth can be found from "all" that is within His eternal, spirit, holy nature. Sins, cheating, stealing, adultery, lust, greed, evil thoughts, killing, robbery, and more such wrongs fall within the human race here on Planet Earth. (Think!) Is this true? This God can only exemplify truth, righteousness and to give opportunity for others to do the same.

These "wrongs" are examples of eternal darkness. Upon the stay of darkness here on Planet Earth, and one found continually in darkness upon their earthly death, then darkness will be their fortress in eternal existence. Darkness here on earth is not equal to the burning lake of fire where there is wailing and gnashing of teeth to all those who dwell there.

This holy, eternal, spirit and everlasting God came into the world here on Planet Earth the usual way to give all an opportunity to receive His light. From this description one could ponder and ask: Which is better, darkness? or light? (twenty-four) seven. Trying to accomplish things in darkness is sometimes impossible. Most want to see what they're doing! Darkness is a void that can be avoided by receiving the gift of eternal life from God. This God is light where there is no darkness! This eternal God is (not maybe) preparing a place (physical) for all who believe and trust in Him (trust and obey). Planet Earth will soon be no more! In times past (approximately a few thousand years ago) Planet Earth was destroyed by a flood of water. At this time all inhabitants (human race only) were found dead except for a few people of one family who decided to (trust and obey) and jump into the boat. This family, about eight in number, replenished the earth, as it is today. One could say: "Glad they jumped in." Earth's final frontier (future) will be destroyed by fire. All occupants of life and material substances will return to dust, whence they came. Faith is needed within oneself to believe these pre- and post-events of Planet Earth's comings and goings. This God wrote that this pre-event (earth flooded by water did happen) and this God wrote (past tense) that Planet Earth will be destroyed by fire. Faith is needed that these events did happen and are going to happen.

God's plan for you is to have all your "wrongs" given to Him for His righteousness sake. Sounds too good to be true! You give Him your wrongdoings being found in darkness and you'll receive His truths, His ways, His eternal life. Yes! This is just the beginning..., realizing at this moment in time (here on Planet Earth only) you've accepted (past tense) the gift of grace from your Creator, you are now saved! Saved from what? Eternal existence, where there are no exit doors, you're alone, found in darkness, hot fiery flames burning the body edgily, scorching heat, body is itching, and God's wrath is now unfolding, the spiritual war is over and all ungenerated spirits are receiving their eternal sentences.

What's next? **For you**! By accepting his gift of eternal life your Creator, the holy, eternal, spirit God is now preparing a place for you in the new heaven, new earth, new universe, new galaxies, far, far away from Planet Earth. All of these new places will be known to you from receiving His gift of eternal life immediately upon your earthly death.

God's knowledge of this earth, planets, people, animals and everything is beyond human comprehension. Since He created everything for Himself by Himself, one could believe He knows everything! He (knows your thoughts before you think) (knows your answers before you speak). Wow! For it is written, "Knows the amount of sand (in pieces) on the seashore, has given each star in the galaxies a name." "You," your past, present, future events, every word you've spoken, all words you ever will speak, every thought, word or deed, this God knows "all" before it is going to happen and how it will happen. Above "all," most important, knows "all" who will accept His gift of eternal life and those who enter eternal existence. **(Remembering faith is needed to please Him), which is the only entrance requirement to see Him as He is.**

It's been a few thousand years since God himself walked on the earth. While God was here for a short time he carried out His mission and defeated the evil, demonic spirit empire by carrying a heavy burden on his back. These heavy, bloody, splintery, wooden timbers were carried by Him because no other could carry it to relieve the wrongful burdens of the evil, demonic, spirit empire. This was done (past tense) so you will (not maybe) have (present tense) eternal life with Him. This Planet Earth god is a spirit (a spirit with no body) which can speak (with words) to this holy, eternal spirit God, knows of its defeat and eternal destruction of His demonic empire setting at eternal existence. **Soon this spiritual war will be over**.

This holy eternal God is creating a new heavenly place for all those (human race only) people who believe in Him. From an earthly perspective it's been in the building process for (two thousand earth years). Earth was created by Him in six days. (What an accomplishment!) Everything you see, touch, feel, smell, taste and all things that you cannot, were created in six days by this eternal God. What a magnificent job! A total piece of art, so brilliant that most people don't believe this was done by this God. The water, land, air, animals, planets, spirits, galaxies and more were created by this God in six (twenty-four hour) days or in one hundred forty-four hours. Wow! Now the best is yet to come. God created human spirits to be just like He is. Yes!

God describes the new heaven where there is **no blood, sweat or tears** and each who dwell there (for eternity) will have a personal relationship with Him. Are you thinking of any questions you might want to ask? "Ask and you'll receive." The materials of this new heavenly construction will be of gold, pearls, diamonds, precious metals (not known to man) that need no fixing. This construction will take place in completion by the voice of God. When God speaks

81

for the construction to begin "all" will be complete when the final words are spoken.

The land area of heaven is so vast that the measurements are not given. The new earth, heaven, galaxies, universe, stars, planets and more are currently under wisdom, intelligence construction. This construction and dwelling place is being built for all those people (earth residents only) of times past, present and future who put their faith in this holy, eternal spirit God.

This is the ultimate gift God is giving for you. Your gift toward this God is to accept this gift which will be a gift given back to God. Remember that you are a created spirit encapsulated in a human body. **You are a spirit and that is all you ever will be.** Today you need to use your free will to determine who you'll put your eternal faith in. Two choices: the eternal, holy spirit God or the god of eternal existence. The holy, eternal, spirit God's plan is to have you with Him in heaven upon the blink of an eye of your earthly death. For it is written, "Once to die when the judgment."

CHAPTER TEN

PROPHECIES

Prophecy, by its own definition, is to predict future happenings that are going to happen. Several textbooks of old day describe happenings that are going to happen before they happen. These individual books, approximately (sixty-six) in number were written over thousands of years by a variety of authors: (most) if not all never knew each other. Simply put, these authors wrote through the inspiration from the holy, eternal, spirit God. These books today are all clustered together referred by a few, as the words of God. From the English language this book (singular) was the first book printed from old day languages to English. This book was written early in the sixteenth century by orders from a king (a ruler over his people). When the king ordered these writings to happen they did and as of year two thousand and six these writings are now circulated worldwide.

This book is the number one book for circulation, most read, often talked about, more prints, most accurate, prophecies foretold (all came true) prophecies to come. Explains where you've been, where you're going, how long you'll live (only estimating), how to live, what your life is worth? How good you are? Life after death, chosen for eternity, describes nature, gods mentioned, catastrophes, famines, earthquakes, floods, lovers of man, fire, one-third blood spill earth, one-third sun darken, one-third moonlight darken, one-third sea animals **lives** spoiled, one-third air **live** decayed, one-third land animals dead, one-third planets burnt, increasing infestations; then from a command the angelic spirits destroy all the earth.

You were prophesied long ago before there was time and space. Your thoughts, words and deeds that you have done, are going to do, are doing, been prophesied and are taking place each day of your life. Consider this, you're an important person! The holy, eternal, everlasting God (who created you) knows your step, every word, every heartbeat, every joy, every curse, every internal organism, every gesture, it is safe to say, this God knows everything but... did not have to learn anything. This God knows everything at all times, past, present and future happenings about you. Today, right now, for you to choose light vs. darkness, truth vs. lies; best, of all, eternal life, worst of all eternal existence. Your will, will?

The flood, the rain, the boat, the people, the animals, the laughter, the criticism, the death, the hope, the beginning, the end, the ride, the land, the bird, the sea, and the rainbow were all prophesied thousands of years by many people before the happening. The exact day or year is not recorded, not important, just that this flood was occurring and that no land was found until forty days passed, by then the rain stopped. Imagine, many rainstorms since but always relief in sight when the rain dribbled its last drop. Back then during this prophesied flood of water covering the highest peak, tallest mountain, there was rain, rain, rain, pouring rain. The sun not shining, no land to be found, no people from outside the boat alive, while these severe rainstorms occurred. No more laughter, no more criticism, no more housing, streets, villages, towns, maps, and all wicked evil man – women were drowned, put to death for their own beliefs and unrepentant way of living.

The boat size (approximately) was about fifty yards wide by one hundred yards long and about forty yards high. What a size! This boat in the making took about one hundred and twenty years and was built mostly of timbers of wood. During this time of building the boat there was a man who found grace in the ways of this holy, eternal, spirit God. This man spoke to this God (voice to voice) in his native language when this God spoke to this man. The conversation that took place in recorded history was mostly about the wicked, demonic generation of people practicing lust, greed, adultery, fornication, lovers of themselves, who (all) turned away from their holy God. (History does have a way of repeating itself.)

Chop, chop, cut, cut, saw, saw, measure, measure, build, build, was the plan of this old age man and his family. Jokes, jokes, laughter, laughter, criticize, criticize, fealth, fealth, as all of those who practice wicked, demonic ways got their pleasure toward this man and his family. This man spoke to all a flood was coming that no one has ever experienced before. So severe of a flood that no land could be seen and all human life would die who were captured by the flood. The crowd of people enjoyed their drunkenness, sexual pleasures, lived without rule of law, sicknesses were rapid, famines, stealing, murders, slaves of lust, and many corruptible practices were found with disbelief that this man could prophecy a flood was coming. The entire crowd through their **free will** chose themselves vs. the holy, eternal, spirit God's way.

Drip, drip, wet, wet, splash, splash, rain, rain, thunder, thunder, lightning, lightning, dark, dark with forty continuous pouring rain, twenty-four hours a day. The boat lifted up from the ground below. Only a few people entered the boat with a count of eight. More known animals entered within than the count of people. The pouring rain continued for forty days and during such time there was no land to view. All people, land animals who did not enter the boat were dead. A rainbow first appeared in the clearing skies toward the end of the forty days of thunderous, pouring rain. This rainbow as it still appears today is a mystery to fellow man on how this can be formed but it is a sign from this God that the earth will never flood again from water. While the people got off the boat from a high mountain it was up to them to multiply and fill the earth's population to this very day.

There are catastrophic prophecies of earth's nature toward fellow man. Earthquakes are rapidly occurring as it is written will happen. The land opens and rapidly closes faster than a blink of an eye and encloses all in its path within the earth's crust. Whatever is nearby – people, structures – earthquakes swallow them up, now inside the earth. No one knows the day, hour or year when earthquakes will occur, just that they are foretold will occur. Earthquake prophecies are occurring on all continents and within bodies of water. These events will continue as it has been given foretold for thousands of years.

Lovers of men/women is a prophecy that has been foretold. This prophecy is not new and has been around here on Planet Earth since the beginning of time. With today's technology of communications, much information is provided without being at the scene of this prophecy. Men marrying men and women marrying women (happening worldwide) is becoming more practiced as of the year two thousand and six. One needs to ponder, is this the right or wrong thing to do? **Let's consider the facts and nothing but the facts**: Of the world's population of approximately five billion (during year two thousand and six) people, let's consider everyone (all) will practice this behavior. Remembering all men will be with all men and all women will be with all women. Being fruitful and multiplying the earth's population will cease. Year after year will pass by, men and women will be only with the other. Days, years pass by, people die. The five billion people are decreasing in number. Why? Under this behavior of sin it's impossible to be fruitful and multiply the human race. Now knowing the average human race life span is three score plus ten (seventy years), the five billion people will all die and the human race will be no more. Is lovers of men/women correct? Now that's the question?

The prophecy of wars seems to be without end. Of all the known wars where the dead are counted and numbered, the total who have died is approximately five billion. This number is equal (approximately) to the number of people living on Planet Earth during the year two thousand and six. Since the beginning of time (exact date unknown) when men/women inhabit the earth there have been wars. Some wars are of the immediate family, other wars are: city-town wars, between states, countries, provinces, nations, religions, governments, national and international wars, and then....., the number "one" spiritual war, currently happening and is the longest war (earth-time-wise) is between two: the holy eternal, spirit God vs. the evil, demonic, spirit earth god. Wars at the end, people die.

The weapons created to fight during these wars have all been used. Each weapon of all types, to the simple, to the most complex (weapons of mass destruction) are, have been and will be used in the future. The human spiritual war of hope is only found from the holy, eternal, spirit God where the end of this war is now known: eternal life or eternal, endless existence. You can participate and be on the winning side!

Famines/diseases are on the increase rapidly during this day of history. These prophecies have been foretold for centuries and are now in our midst worldwide. Man, with his rapid knowledge of technology, medicines, full treatments are still not found for these. Why? is most often asked! The correct answer, because fallen man is cursed and continually falls away from the holy eternal God. God's way or man's way, you need to decide. Remembering your free will is making a decision for you right now. God's ways are for truth, justice, giving, and all things are possible for the entrance of eternal life. Man's way (you pick the man) (plenty to choose from) all equal to one place: the entrance to eternal existence where there are no exits (**only deposits, no returns**). With all the diseases (more to come), famines (are forever happening) the cures are simple: "I will (not maybe) bless those who bless Me or I will curse those who curse Me," equals no more famines or diseases.

The prophecy of the holy, eternal, spirit God's wrath has been told more times than most stories. Years ago (approximately two thousand years) the man who claimed to be God explained in precise, exact details of his holy God's wrath. Using the word (God's) needs to be explained at this time. The holy, eternal, heavenly spirit God is "One" that always exists that no person will ever see. This is simple to understand because you cannot see a spirit. This God **self-sustains** Himself without using any kind of energy. This God is the Creator of all things spiritual and material. The God of eternal heaven is a spirit God that again the human race will never see. Spirits are beings without bodies (like you). The man who claims to be God is the same as the heavenly spirit God and the holy eternal spirit God the Creator of all things. The holy, eternal, spirit God temporarily took on a human body to communicate with us (the human race). This man you could see, touch, feel and listen to and believe that He is God of all things spiritual and material. All three Gods are the same with only different ways to communicate with their creation (fellow man). The man who claims to be God explains in details (precise) the prophecy of God's wrath to come. This wrath is occurring daily for the demonic (fallen) angelic spirits. The free will unsaved human spirits prophecy of God's wrath is occurring daily here on earth and upon entrance of eternal existence. The prophecy of God's eternal life **is yours for the taking for you just to do the asking**.

The prophecy of God's wrath began early in man's/woman's life of old day. At this time only two humans inhabited the earth: a male and a female. Both choosing darkness of their wrongs over truthful light. At this time for the both of them they were told they were going to die. This was the beginning of God's death wrath as it is written, "**Death entered the human race**."

God's prophecy wrath toward the earth animals vs. the human race is continuing from day one to this present day. Most all animals will attack and kill the human race for their daily food. Humans: Watch out!

From the complex tiny bug that bites, the lions that devour and snakes that poison are all under God's wrath of prophecy toward fellow men. This curse from God's wrath where animals eat one another will continue without end.

God's prophecy of wrath, nature vs. the human race is on the rise compared to centuries or even thousands of years ago. Simple reasoning, to God's nature wrath towards fellow man is because the human population is increasing. More of nature's wrath by God is because more and more people are turning away from this holy, eternal God. Remembering God's way of truthful living vs. man's ways of wrongful living: You decide?

Is the sun getting hotter? Or is it cooling off? The waters getting cleaner or slowly becoming polluted? The air is sparkling clean or is it: cough, cough? The winds, the seas, oceans, land masses, the trees, grasses, the planets, solar system and universe are slowly trying to capture men/women in eternal existence upon their earthly death. So now one can ponder to determine God's wrath of nature towards the human race is slowly consuming occupants in eternal existence.

The holy, eternal, spirit, heaven God's prophecy wrath of the evil one and all fallen demonic spirits from heaven where eternal existence will be their destiny. Each and every demonic spirit knows the eternal end and how it was in the beginning. These demonic spirits which can speak to one another know the eternal end for them is near as this has been foretold to all openly. The new setting in eternal existence for these evil spirits will be: secluded, alone, no communication with any other, little or no movements, memories well intact, no escape, pains, pains, pains... and being consumed in the lake of fire. All of the demonic spirits, one-third fallen evil spirits and all of the unsaved human spirits who through their "free will" reject the holy, eternal, spirit God's grace, have been foretold of their eternal existence destiny.

There is a prophecy of the holy, eternal, spirit God's judgment of the human race. For it is written, "Once you'll die then the judgment." What? That's right! A judgment is coming soon for all spirits. **Remember you are a spirit who has temporarily taken on a human body**. Your body will soon return to the earth from whence it came but your spirit will last forever. Upon one's earthly death a judgment occurs from your Creator. The judgment will be for all those spirits of the human race and all those demonic spirits who through their own free will chose to reject, defame the holy, eternal, spirit, everlasting God. It could be said, "You reject me, I'll reject you, your choice." This judgment will take place one spirit at a time with only the holy, eternal, spirit God present during that spirit being judged. (This prophecy currently occurring: daily.) This judgment will occur where there are no time clocks, defense attorneys, juries; just the spirit being judged by the holy, eternal, spirit God! This judgment from an earthly perspective will be over "faster than a blink of an eye." The verdict of the judgments will be: **"eternal life" or "eternal existence."**

A present-day prophecy from this God is that His word will be spread to all people of every tongue and all land areas of Planet Earth. To accomplish this task you need people who will be servants and a written instrument that can be read with clear, precise details, everything about this holy God. From the beginning of time (exact date unknown) to this present day, this prophecy is happening. Let's see how it works!

The earliest known man and woman who inhabited the earth, this holy eternal God spoke to them. The conversation was first an introduction among themselves and then God gave them certain instructions to do and not to do. Man/woman (back then) like today chose their way vs. God's way. From that moment on till this present day, the human race is discovering God's wrath. So, from that time in the beginning God spoke His words, from His voice, to start the "**good news**" for the human race. Centuries have passed, God's words, God's voice is continually being spoken and understood only by a few. His words of times past, present and future are and will be written down in a form of a text so "all," "everyone" (human spirits) only will know who He is and why He came to Planet Earth.

Now you can read and remember this holy God's word reaching down to proclaim to the human race that He is the way, the truth and the life. God's wrath for the evil one, demonic angelic spirits and all other spirits who chose to rebel against him will have an ending without Him. **Warnings! Warnings! Warnings! <u>Red flags</u>, <u>red flags</u>,** and more <u>**red flags**</u> are posted throughout Planet Earth to avoid being captured by the evil one. The holy, eternal, spirit God can and will be your best friend now and for all eternity or this God will be your very worst enemy. Your free will, will? God's glory streets of gold, prophesied or an abundance of fire on your brow, prophesied.

The prophecy, "the book." Foretold for centuries and is now defined, clearly written, distributed on all continents, number "one" published book of all times, written for you, explains more than six hundred sixty individual prophecies, past prophecies, prophecies presently happening and future prophecies. Prophecies of where you've been, where you're going, when you were born, when you're going to die. The prophecy of the afterlife, what to do during your life here on Planet Earth, who knows you best and the prophecy of who created you are all written down from this number "one" text of all times.

The prophecy of love, justice, judgments, and eternal life and eternal existence are clearly explained. This text is the first book written in the English language. This book provides detailed information about the new earth, new heaven (currently under construction), new universe, new galaxies, new names given in eternal life (one name per person) and....... more!

This prophecy book tells you why you're here on Planet Earth (to receive the gift of eternal life). This book tells you how you're supposed to live and your only purpose of why you're living. This book provides information when you're going to die, then a joyful or torture judgment. This book explains where your body and eternal spirit goes upon your last breath on earth. This book tells you who you are as a person and how good you are. The why? how? when? where? and who? are all answered clearly about eternity that no other book provides this information. You! Yes, you have access to this book 24/7 (twenty-four-seven)! "Ask and thou shalt receive." Not maybe, but shall!

This book, written by many different authors, written without errors, page by page, chapter by chapter. This book explains everything about the past, present and future (without mistakes or cross-outs or maybes). The exhausted time of writing took thousands of years to complete, as the last chapter states, "It is finished!" The writings of this book, without the use of copying machines, computers, proper lighting, sharing information with others for accuracy, took place in "old days," and is still used during the year of two thousand and six (during this text writing).

This book is a collection of individual books totaling sixty-six in number, put together to form a complete set of the holy, eternal, spirit God's words of: **Why you were born?** and the only purpose of your life! This text (the only one that exists) explains everything in graphic, precise details with one hundred percent accuracy. There are no "best" words that describe that this holy, eternal, spirit God exists, just that He does exist for you. Now you can say, **"Someone wrote a book for me."**

CHAPTER ELEVEN

<u>ANGELS</u>

How many angels are there? What is an angel? Where are they and what are they doing? The words from an angel, yes! Angels can speak and speak often. Some angels speak truths which are guided by the holy, eternal, spirit God, and others speak trickery, deceit, lust, evil, corruption, and all ungodliness against their Creator.

Angels are spirits (without bodies). Hard to imagine from an earthly perspective, but true. Heavenly angels who reside in heaven have something that you have. All angels have a "free will" to practice truths or enter into evil corruption. The human race can practice truths or enter into evil corruption, too! You have what angels don't have. That is, you have a body that people can see, touch, feel, listen and talk to. **Remember you are a living spirit that has temporarily taken on a human body**. That's right! All angels who reside in heaven have one thing in common with another and that is they were created (from nothing) to serve the holy, eternal, spirit God. These heavenly angels communicate directly with their Creator on moment by moment intervals. Here on Planet Earth the clock is ticking, the sun rises, the sun sets, it's dark, it's light, and having this it's difficult to imagine angelic beings not having the same. These angelic beings are busy serving their Creator. They do such tasks as: traveling the universe, galaxies, going to and fro Planet Earth, where you are, where you live, work, play and communicate with others, angelic spirits are there (watching you). In times past these heavenly angelic beings have communicated to fellow man by speaking, to explain the "how," "why," "where," and "who" message from their Creator. It could be said, "These angelic beings are proper (spokesmen) and are only servants."

How many angelic spirit beings are there? At one time of recorded history angelic beings outnumbered the human race. One man, one woman, in the beginning adds up to two. During this time of earth's history, one-third (1/3) of all evil, demonic, angelic spirits were cast out of heaven and entered time and space here on Planet Earth. A multitude (numbers unknown) of these evil, angelic spirits who resided in the most "high" heavenly place are now in our midst causing corruption to all they encounter. These angelic spirit beings "who" all had conversations with their Creator of what to do, and how to do it, now are all eventually doomed for <u>eternal existence</u>.

As the human population increases in number the angelic spirit beings remain the same. As of two thousand six, the human population is about five billion people – wow! Compared to about four or five thousand years ago (exact date unknown) there was only one man and one woman who entered a "time zone;" that is, time lapsed for the both of them. It could be said, **"Time was no longer on their side."** The clock started to tick and both of them fell to death into the earth from whence they came. The one third evil, demonic angelic beings who are the "masters" of evil doings, corruption and evil ways toward the human race continue to practice their crafts today, trying to increase the population of <u>eternal existence</u>. As time marches on, all these demonic, angelic spirits here on Planet Earth will always continue to rebel against their Creator.

These evil angelic beings can and are corrupting the animals that inhabit the earth. At one moment of time near the beginning, these evil angelic spirits cursed one animal to lie and crawl on its belly all the days of their life. Imagine, you having a free will to choose: God's ways vs. evil, demonic ways, truths vs. tell lies and eventually entering eternal life with your Creator or entering eternal existence with all evil spirits, your will, will?

The angelic beings, good or evil, all have individual names. One name for each angelic being given by their Creator. Of all the names people have, many have the same first, last and middle names. These names, some are spelled the same, others have different letters, different pronunciations, so that many can have the same name even though they're different people. The angelic beings "all" have individual names (one per angelic being). This is true like the stars of the universe (possibly billions of stars) all have one name per star given by this holy, eternal, spirit God.

The saved human spirits who, upon their death, enter the holy, eternal kingdom of heaven will have angelic spirits as their servants. How many angelic heavenly spirits are there for the saved spirits of the human race? (Unknown.) At eternal life in heaven all angelic spirits will be servants of the human race spirits. This happening will be for all eternity. You can ponder from an earthly perspective what you want these angelic spirits to do for you? Imagine! The new heaven, earth, galaxies, universes, planets, stars and more (currently under construction): without corruption, evil demonic angelic spirits, day or night, no sleep, no resting, no waiting, it's time to have hope that these events are truthful for those who enter eternal life.

Angels are servants of the holy, eternal spirit God who will escort the saved human spirits through the entrance of the new heaven. This will occur for the human saved spirits, without asking! The saved human spirits upon entrance will receive a new name (one per person), a new eternal body (that won't decay), and there's a mansion being constructed for the believers in Him (the holy, eternal God). Sounds too good to be true! **"Greater are those (human race only) who believe, yet have not seen, than those who had to see in order to believe."**

Angelic spirit beings of evil corruption and those truthful, guided angelic spirits are both here on Planet

Earth. The saved souls (believers in Him, singular) have (present tense) an angelic spirit that is assigned to each believer. Wow! Yes, it's true! This angelic spirit serves, guides, corrects and informs only truths in the lives of the believer. The unsaved souls of the human race (from their free will) are slowly being captured by the one-third evil, demonic spirits who play a role in their lives to divert their attention away from the gift of eternal life.

In recorded history some of these truthful angelic spirits have taken on a human body to serve the will of their holy God. Eyewitnesses have seen these events, wrote them down in texts and are being told for centuries since their origin. These truthful angelic spirits outnumber the evil, demonic spirit angels two to one. This spiritual war has been going on for thousands of years (exact date unknown) prior to the creation of the human race.

This angelic spiritual war of truths vs. evil has only one thing in common. When this spiritual war ends (nobody) dies spiritually because all spirits created by the one, true, everlasting, holy, eternal spirit will experience eternity, just depending upon where? Each angelic spirit knows each other's name. Each angelic spirit knows your name, each angelic spirit knows time is not on their side. Each angelic spirit knows the holy, eternal, spirit God personally. Each angelic spirit knows of eternal life or eternal existence (where the worm eats and dieth not). **What are you going to do? What are you going to do? What are you going to do? When the angelic spirits come for you?**

CHAPTER TWELVE

MIRACLES

Miracles by definition are events which occur without an explanation of how or why they happen. Miracles from day one on Planet Earth to this day are happening. Miracles are happening without many people knowing because communications are not directed toward them. It has been often said, "Now that's a miracle," "It will be a miracle if I win." Miracles, miracles and more miracles are occurring each day but many go unnoticed or not claimed by anyone. Recorded miracles are found in numerous texts to indicate truths for the human race from a man who claims to be God.

From a common-sense point of view without being highly educated or having any education at all, consider nature as a miracle. The planets orbiting to and from each different from another are miracles. Each planet has a cause or a plan for something to guide the earth its correct path. The planet sun has many miracles within its energy force. This energy directly affects Planet Earth. The sun's distance from Planet Earth because it has been said, "That a few million miles further or closer," the earth would be covered with ice or burnt out. This equals to no life of any nature on Planet Earth, which is a miracle.

The earth's "degrees" of rotation toward its neighboring planets is a miracle. A few "degrees" higher or lower, the following could occur: possibly no more land, the water would engulf the land masses, the four seasons would be one and possibly the weather temperature could be zero. With the "degrees" pitch another angle the temperatures everywhere would be higher than that of the equator. Now that's a miracle that this is not happening.

The earth's animal life is a miracle. How many different animals are there? (Unknown.) Not important! Each animal has a purpose to sustain human life. Without the animals where would food, clothing, medicines and protection for the human race be? (Uncertain.) Yes, the animals of water, air and land are needed one for another for the existence of fellow man. The only difference between man/woman being an animal and all other animals is that the human race has an eternal spirit. This spirit lasts forever. All other animals have no spirits and upon their life expectancy they all die without an afterlife. The human race has dominion over the animal kingdom.

You can have eternal life which is a miracle. The spirits of the human race will exist forever. Your "free will" determines where, eternal life or eternal existence, your spirit will enter. This is a miracle that is given to you freely. **What do you have to do to enter eternal life**? Accept this gift from the giver who is this holy, eternal, spirit God. **What do you have to do to enter eternal existence? Nothing!**

The miracle gift from a man who claims to be God offers freely his miracle of eternal life. Such a miracle gift that only takes a belief in Him to receive eternal life. This miracle was prophesied thousands of years ago and is believed today only by a few. This man performs miracles such as: walking on water, curing fatal diseases, having the crippled walk, the blind to see, calm the storm, raise the dead to life, raise Himself out of the grave of death ("out from the grave He arose") during His time on Planet Earth.

Miracles, miracles and more miracles there are but the most important miracle is: **You**. There is no other person like you, no other person looks like you. Your talents, thoughts, words, deeds, color, skin texture, fingerprints, DNA identification and more are all yours and yours alone. The most important miracle is to receive the gift of eternal life from this holy, eternal spirit God. With Him it is written, "You can have (present tense) life more abundantly." You want more? You want eternal life? You want this miracle? <u>Your will, will</u>?

CHAPTER THIRTEEN

<u>REVELATION</u>

Revelation by this definition is: (astonishing events that will occur: <u>prophesied</u>, that will be witnessed) till the end of time. You are a revelation! You are participating in revelations. You were born at this time in revelation. You are witnessing revelation unfolding rapidly. You will be entering a no time zone revelation (no time left for you). Some say, "There's not enough time to do what I want to do," "Don't worry be happy," soon time will be no more. "<u>Worry</u>" about eternal existence, be "<u>happy</u>" about eternal life. "Don't worry be happy!"

These revelations are occurring and will occur with and without notice: earthquakes, famines, violet storms, ocean rising to high depths, governments rising and rapidly falling, followers of man, animal, planets and material gods, one world government, one world money system, one world god, one world war, holy angels destroying the earth and all of its inhabitants, no more moons, planets or earth, a bloody earth filled, one world religion, inextinguishable fire, the sun will lose its light, a trial of the century occurs, a judgment and sentence of all unsaved human spirits, a judgment and sentence of all demonic, angelic spirits, rewards for the saved human spirits on judgment day, remember every knee will bow: the saved and unsaved human spirits, the demonic and angelic spirits to the holy, eternal, spirit God! Revelations of eternal life or eternal existence are present and more!

Astonishing revelation events are currently occurring on Planet Earth that people are observing. These events, like violent storms of water affecting all continents and standards of living. Storms of water rising in footage of more than fifty feet of vertical height. Storms crushing boating, sinking the unsinkable ships and airplanes of travel flee its force. These storms enter the land area with such speed and force that everything within its direction is destroyed or dead.

How and why these storm events happen go unanswered from an earthly perspective. The unsaved spirits of man/woman only have their educational guess of why these violet, tragic, deathly storms happen. All in all their guesses are wrong. So many theories of each event are changed or altered that no truth can be found. These tragic events happen to give people notice that Planet Earth is for the here and now, not for the future.

Revelations of earthquakes on land, water and icy land areas are happening in every direction of the compass. On a moment's notice the land area opens, shifts, moves direction then closes within seconds! Whatever is within its path is totally enclosed into the earth's crust. People, animals, ice, water, land, vegetation and other elements gone, dead totally devastated. Earthquakes are a mystery of how, why or where the next quakes will be. This revelation of earthquakes will occur and continue till the end of time on Planet Earth.

The revelation of famines by definition is when there is no enough food or water to feed a portion of the human race. This revelation includes animal life, too. At this year (two thousand and six years) more and more famines are occurring. It has been said by the man who claims to be God, "I will (not maybe) curse those who curse me," or "Bless those who bless me." This could be an example of an "eye for an eye" or a "tooth for a tooth." So one can ponder within the famine areas of the world are they cursing or blessing the man who claims to be God? Religions, gods and more gods exist on Planet Earth where people (all) have a free will choose one. To choose darkness gods equals entrance to eternal existence or the God who will bless you now and forever in eternal life is the choice of only a few.

Violent storms across the oceans and across the continents are continuing more frequently than ever. Today's technology of communication advertises these advents as their happening. Today's date and time of history is when revelations are occurring. Revelations of rainstorms, hailstorms, snowstorms, and all violent storms are cursing the animal and human life. Hailstorms with hail falling to the earth in two to three inches in diameter causing severe damage. When these pieces of hail hit buildings, structures or land areas, total destruction takes place. The rapid movement of hail falling from the sky hitting animals and human life at times death occurs. This revelation is happening most times without warning!

Ocean areas, within seconds, rising to heights of twenty-five feet without any warning is a revelation occurring during this day of history. This creates huge waves of water which destroy all in its path. When landing toward the shore the land, vegetation, and structures most times are destroyed. People, animal life, buildings, structures, traveling apparatus and normal ways of living are totally wiped out, gone! People, animal life now dead. The inner land structures wash away into the ocean or are placed to permanent distances away from their origin. People, governments, nations or nature are not the cause of this revelation. These elements are causing destruction to human life and the normal way of living.

Governments rising, falling and trying to dominate the other, until there's a one world government on Planet Earth, is a revelation that is mostly untold. This revelation began on day one of Planet Earth's human inhabitants and will continue until there will be a one world government. (Pause and ponder), is this revelation true? Are there current (year two thousand eight) evidences to support this?

Governments, dictators, kings, queens, tribes, chiefs and other ways to govern the human race all have failed or are failing. This revelation will continue without success until a one world leader (singular), a (male) appears to government the entire world under his rule of law. What this male leader will do, **"Try and calm the storm,"** but as the story and his leadership unfolds the end will be "wailing and gnashing of teeth" in eternal existence for all who surrender!

Followers of man gods, animal gods, planet gods, material gods, Planet Earth god, angelic gods, demon gods, satanic gods, a man who claims to be God, other gods, or no gods are more popular today than ever before. Most people fall into at least one of these revelations.

CHAPTER FOURTEEN

GODS (PLURAL) AUTOBIOGRAPHY

There are at least four known autobiographies of the one, true, holy, eternal God. Since the beginning of time (exact date unknown) the human race talk, spoke to, observe, listen, and witness this plural God in their midst. When this God spoke, people listen. Numerous times throughout history people (only a few) talk to their Creator. Your imagination needs to unfold at this time if you were one of those persons who talk to the voice of God without seeing His face: What would you have done? or what were you doing to have this voice of God talk to you? Those happenings occurred in old days and up to a couple of thousand years ago. Written testimonies are found on who did the talking and about the conversations that took place. **Today your voice can (not maybe) talk to this God** and <u>**there will be a response**</u> that the message got through! It is written from these autobiographies that you can or someday you will (not maybe) have (present tense) a conversation with this God. This will occur for all eternity or have a brief conversation (possibly only seconds) then enter eternal existence.

The story about this eternal God is: He always was, always will be, and in the beginning He created all things material and spiritual.

This God self-sustains Himself and knows everything from the first to the last. His words are His words, His interests are His interests, answers to Himself, His truths are His truths, His ways are His ways, His forgiveness is His forgiveness, His judgments are His judgments, His wraths are His wraths, His grace is for Himself, His eternal life is His eternal life and His eternal existence is His eternal existence.

Of the four known writers of these (plural) God's autobiography, most told the same story. All of these writers or authors have this in common with the other: All spoke to this God! All walk with Him and witness miracles by Him. All encountered a personal relationship with Him. All are (present tense) with Him today in eternal life. All saw Him walk on water, answer all questions asked of Him. He spoke words that only He was God. All writers of his God's nature, their spirits entered eternal life. All knew or witnessed His death. They witnessed Him rise from dead to life. All received gifts, talents to perform miracles using His name. They taught many other believers (in Him) to do the same. All believed in Him for eternal life. All witness "Him" cure the blind to see, the lame to walk, the diseased persons to be cured and all witnessed His story of eternal existence of the spirit/body or eternal life with Him.

These writers wrote with clarity, with such details that their writings have not changed for substance in more than two thousand years! As they wrote their story of this plural God they did not confirm their writings to the other. They just wrote and left it to the reader to believe or not to believe!

The first writer (the exact date unknown) wrote in his autobiography, in the beginning was this God. This makes "good sense" because if this God appeared after the beginning, during the beginning or somewhere else, His truths that he is the only God would fail. Fail not! Because in the beginning He is, was, and always will be. Most interesting that during this God's travel in time and space on Planet Earth He (God) needed to explain His purpose in life. This God first came to acknowledge man by His voice. For hundreds and thousands of years only His voice was heard to indicate to fellow man that there is a God. Fellow man/woman was not alone on Planet Earth.

The first man/woman heard the voice of God then spoke to God.

The conversations that took place during those times were to inform them the way to righteousness. Their free will chose a path of wrongdoings that ultimately found their death. One could ponder that the first man and woman on Planet Earth would understand death and the death penalty to enter eternal existence? The second thought would be if they (man/woman) even understood life! The evidence unfolds that the first man and woman spoke (using their words) to God and clearly understood their purpose in life.

Their purpose was to communicate, learn eternal truths and to forever know why they were created. This process of knowing why they were created took many hundreds of years for them to understand. (One could say they're slow learners.) This plural God is patient and wants the **belief in Him** so that **none will perish to eternal existence**.

From the early years of their lives when they both met (God and this man), both were in human bodies. Now (plural God's) voice took on a human body. At this time, approximately two thousand years ago, people now could see, touch, feel, listen and observe this God 24/7 to eyewitness His identity. It was written from old ancient texts approximately two to four thousand years ago that this God would be born to conquer the wrath of man. To consider why thousands and thousands of years passed before God took on a human body is quite simple: "Remembering God's ways are not man's ways," as most people think.

So now this plural God is among us. From an infant to a young adult God is now here. Proof, proof, proof that this infant was, is, God, needs to be explained by God Himself. Keep it plain, make it simple, mention no lies as this God has His purpose for the human race.

From His early youth (probably before his teenage years) leaders of the community, government officials, heads of worship, town folk and average everyday working people listened to His mastery knowledge of all the old ancient texts. Verse by verse, He knew them all.

The people heard His truths as this God spoke openly in public. All were amazed, at such a young age how this information could be obtained within Himself. Verse by Verse, chapter by chapter, word by word He spoke as if He was reading from the texts. The crowds gathered closer and became eyewitnesses to these words He spoke that He was the only way to eternal life. The crowd talked among themselves asking another: How can such a young lad recite these passages without going to school? How can someone speak with such authority? What gave Him permission to enter conversations to others with authority? The answers are quite simple: God's ways, not man's ways! **Eternal life or eternal existence for the human spirits**. (That's the answer given.)

(Plural) God's needs to be defined at this time so no confusion takes place for all. The human race has an eternal spirit within their body. Faith needs to enter your thoughts to believe that this is true! This plural God has an eternal spirit, a human body and describes He is the eternal God of heaven. During His life here on earth this God temporarily took on a human body. Now this plural God is with us! He declared to all mankind that they and He (present tense) has an eternal spirit within the body. At this time it is known of this God that He is a spirit and now has a human body. More proof is needed during His life that as He and others declared, He is the holy, eternal, spirit God, Creator of all things material and spiritual.

The evidences are that He is who He says He is are: The prophecy and location of His birth, miracles He performed, His death and bodily resurrection to life. Eyewitnesses concur these truths. It takes a belief that he has three separate distinct natures: having a human body, second a spirit within his body, and thirdly a belief that He is the Creator of all things material and spiritual. He declared that there is only one, true, holy, eternal God which is Himself. Thus, this plural God has three natures: a spirit here on earth (like you have), a human body (like you have), and thirdly His first identity (a holy, eternal, spirit God) of eternal life which resides in a spiritual place called heaven.

Three separate distinct natures but only one identity. Sounds confusing? Answer yes! Sounds impossible? Answer yes! Sounds like only this eternal, holy, spirit God can do? Answer yes! It's time to ponder and compare all other gods to this plural God. The other gods have this in common with the other: all have no beginning or end, all are dead physically or spiritually, have no explanation of why (you) were born, most all were created by man, have no complete texts to govern man, or have no texts at all and most all do not explain the purpose of man's creation.

History records a few thousand years ago this plural God introduced Himself to mankind only using His voice. Since that time He became a man with His spirit within to conquer the wrath of spiritual death for the human race. This was God's purpose of His life. To make Himself known physically, to conquer the sin wrath of man, to explain with precise details how to enter His eternal life or enter God's wrath of eternal existence. The free will of the human race will choose to believe or not to believe in Him.

The second autobiography of this plural God writes more about God's wrath toward demonic evil spirit, the rebelled angelic spirits, and the unsaved human spirits. God's wrath (currently happening) toward the unsaved spirits are those who enter eternal existence. The vivid description from this author fully describes God's wrath toward evil, sin, lust, greed, pride, boastful creatures, fallen demonic angels and all those of the human race who choose not to accept his gift of eternal life.

Fire, brimstone, wailing, gnashing of teeth, burning, extreme heat, lake of fire, no exists, entry only one way, torture, sweat, perspiration, no food, no drink, no sleep, no talking to others, remembering past, present and future happenings, heat rashes to the body, skin blister pimples, limbs moving inchly, no medicines, no rest, constant torture, old and wrinkly, hot burning skin, completely naked, remembering days past on Planet Earth, remembering endless choices to choose the gift of eternal life, knowing those who choose the gift of eternal life, forever 24/7 hazing, shouting, cursing, pleading, begging for an exit to leave.

This next author writes about this plural God during his time on Planet Earth. An explanation, in great details, is given on what must take place before this God returns to earth for His honor and glory.

During their time together (approximately twenty years) this writer traveled with this God through towns, cities, countries, nations, villages, on oceans, seas and to the outermost parts where people dwell. Many eyewitnesses saw this God in action, in prayer, in sleep, in places of worship, in debates, explaining how to live, where to live, who to live with, where to store your treasures, how to conserve your money, how to treat your neighbor, how to marry, who to marry, why you marry, when to divorce, what to drink, what to eat, when to work, how to work, when not to work, who to love, what not to love, when to love, why you love, and all other questions pertaining to life, eternal existence or eternal life with Him.

Ask this God questions and all questions were answered without error. Ask this God questions today and all questions will be (not maybe) answered with eyewitness results for those who believe in Him.

During this God's life here on earth he traveled mostly with men and women who had a total belief in Him. Some of these travelers had jobs, families and others had none of the same. All of His closest companions with this God had this in common with the other: witness and perform miracles. A miracle by this definition is (an event or an occurrence happening with an intervention by this God causing it to happen or not). They all heard the purpose of why He came to earth, knew where He does dwell, what this God is now doing, (determining eternal life or eternal existence for all spirits). This process by Him is an either-or determination. All of His closest travelers went distances of approximately one hundred miles in land areas of the Far East. This represents only a land area of about one thousand twenty-seven percent of earth's land area.

This writer declared openly to all that he encountered the eternal God. How and why God's own people and government turned against Him. Miracles, miracles and more miracles this God did all for good. The people and government officials witnessed these and then set a plot to kill Him. God Himself knew this from the beginning (exact date unknown, not important) but continued His purpose to witness to all that He is the only God. He and His Father in heaven are one. Sounds confusing? Answer yes! Needs more clarification! So the writer continues:

This plural God, now in human form (having a body) came into the world of time and space on Planet Earth. This purpose was to defeat and conquer spiritual death. This was achieved and witnessed by believers and nonbelievers, eyewitnesses, writings, text from old day and finally from Himself when after dying He returned to life. This spiritual war back then (exact date unknown) continues to this very day. This is a spiritual war to determine a final place to reside for all spirits. This war is between two spiritual beings: one is the Creator of all things material and spiritual known as the holy, eternal, spiritual God, and the other is a created spiritual being known as the god of Planet Earth.

Plural God's nature, truths, all knowing, spoke all languages, knows all things, cured diseases, weather elements obey Him and defeated the earth spirit god

(Satan) Himself by conquering spiritual death. This is plural God's purpose in life and why He was born.

During the end of His journey in life after proclaiming He was the only God, that His kingdom was not of this world, the people and government chose to put Him to death. He did receive a trial, possibly one of the shortest (time-wise) trials of all time. This plural God had no attorney representing Him. During this day and time of history there were lawyers available! The trial (possibly) only an hour in duration where there were no jurors, no appeals of the verdict. The sentence was given by the judge in charge of this court which was to put this man (who claimed to be God) to death.

The sentence was given to this plural/God, a man who claimed to be God, to die one of the most horrific death sentences known to man. This death sentence was common during this time of history (approximately two thousand years ago). To attach a person's body to timbers of wood by nailing the limbs to the wood with ropes securing the body. Once attached, the body (most naked) hanging vertical for all could see the criminal die to their death. No one came off alive!

Prior to this death sentence according to the law of the land the criminal would be chained from their body to a wooden post. This post in height is about the same height of the criminal. Here the criminal is inches away from this wooden, splintery post attached with chains. The criminal's clothing covering would be less than average. The penalty would be to whip the criminal forty lashes with a razor-edge whip, piercing the skin of the criminal. To describe the whip would be as a rough burley piece of long twine (approximately) ten feet long. The edges of the whip would be sharp razor, glass chips of metal along the entire twine. The end of the whip are ball-like attachments with metal piercing needles. The highly skilled whipper would now strike the captive criminal leaning on the post with forty lashes. The criminal's skin, muscles, body parts would be ripped open, torn apart or removed from the body. If the criminal survived the forty whip lashes the law permits, then the criminal would be attached to timbers of wood, hung vertically until death. (Most died at the post!)

The plural/God's body withstood all forty whip lashings during this part of His death sentence. The crowd of the town, some of His closest followers, the government, those in charge of this process watched the horrific terror as this whipping occurred. Whip number one through forty as this plural/God received the severe, horrific pain while His body was torn, ripped open, body parts severed, His blood pouring out over his entire body. At the conclusion of the fortieth whip His body stood vertical unrecognizable to anyone, even his closest followers could not recognize Him. He stood and stood and stood clinging to the old rough, splintery wooden post until the whipping was over. The law permitted not, in excess of forty whip lashes under no conditions.

What's next? The autobiographer writer continues; removing the rough, jagged, bloody chains from His blood-soaked, ripped-open body was done not in tender care! Fast chain release was common. This task was difficult as part of the chain is now inserted in parts of His body. Rip, rip, pull, pull, tear, tear, the chain is now removed from His body. Blood, blood and more blood, torn, ripped-open flesh and body parts, covered His body as all watched. Now comes the final sentence to be hung vertical on pieces of wood until death occurs.

The mocking, the teasing, the shouting, "**Save yourself if you are God!**" The chains were removed and very little garments that were worn, He (God) carried His own timbers of wood to the earth hole. Here they would be inserted with Him (God) attached to them. He (God) was moving the wood timbers towards the earth hole when a mocker from the crowd approached Him. The mocker attached a thorny, prickly crown to His (God's) head, "Look now, he is God with His crown."

Now at the earth hole with the timbers of wood horizontal to the ground the plural/God is being fastened to them. The guards and instructionist are now lying his body horizontal while stretching out His arms left to right. First the ropes are fastened to His arms near His wrist and being fastened near His ankles. Tight, tight, tight, now the body is securely attached to the splintery beams with very little movement.

When rope to the rough, burly, splintery timbers of wood the guards and instructionalist would secure His body by nailing through His hands and feet jagged, old, rusty nails. These old, crusty, blood-stained nails would pierce through the limbs into the wood timbers so the body could not be removed by thyself.

The old, burly, rusty, jagged nails would rest on the skin of his feet and hands. The guards, one holding the nail over the skin, another would swing the heavy pound hammer up high then strike the nail into the skin. Through the skin the nail would go then into the timbers of wood. The body now attached and cannot escape. The extreme pain, torture and anguish of the person is beyond belief. The next nails, similar fashion, would be nailed the same way. One nail per hand, one nail per foot as the pain of insertion is felt.

At this time of nailing this plural/God to the timber of wood was immediately following His forty whip lashings. His body engulfed in blood, skin ripped open, body extremities cut wide open, clothed very little, while this in-pounding nailing process was done. The thorny, prickly, sharp-edged wreath now inserted into His forehead and brow indicating by the crowd that He is God.

Now lifting the wood timbers with His body attached into a deep earth hole came next. Only a portion of the vertical wood timber would be inserted. The government, rulers, town folk and some of His closest followers now watch this blood-soaked, partially clothed, mostly unrecognizable plural/God's death begin.

This death sentence was common for criminals of that day (approximately two thousand years ago). Those criminals commit such horrific, torture crimes that the government believed this death sentence was just. The innocent could now watch this harsh, bloody, torture criminal death for hours, sometimes for days until death occurs. The innocent knew no criminal ever got off those timbers of wood alive!

The plural/God's body now hung on these timbers of wood to die as the crowd looked on. Two other well known, horrific criminals received this death sentence and were placed vertically beside this plural/God's timbers. All three, all hung vertically feet apart from another to slowly die a tortured death. You need to ponder at this time what these proceedings entail. (Possibly be) the criminals' screams, the crowds' cheers as this death sentence often occurred.

The third autobiographer writer continues with a unique conversation that occurred among this plural/God's timber of wood death and the two others that were receiving the same. A criminal to His (God's) left, the other to His right, as conversations among the three were heard from the bystanders. Part of this death sentence the government allowed the criminals to talk as they were not muffled in any way. The conversations varied in nature as one criminal stating: "We (except this plural/Gods) deserve such death punishments because of our horrific crimes. Here, many are witnessing this man/God being put to death for no crimes at all." The plural/God spoke to both and others who were near stating, "**My kingdom is not of this world!**" With that bold statement as He often spoke realize that beyond Planet Earth, its planets, galaxies, universes, their lies this plural/God's kingdom with only one entrance requirement. This will ensure eternity with Him.

Hour after hour as the sun started to set one (attorney criminal) said to this plural/God, forgive me of my criminal deeds as I believe in you (God). With a quick response this plural/God spoke to the entrapped criminal, **"Today you'll be with me in eternal life."** Wow! Such repentance, such forgiveness, such mercy, such grace, such humbleness, such reality, such a place as **eternal life**.

The fourth writer continues in his writings as what happens next! The plural/God's last breath was exhaled as His bodily functions were no more. Eyewitnesses, eyewitnesses and many eyewitnesses saw His body now collapse on the wood timbers without movement. His closest followers and the crowd looked close to see His diaphragm not inhaling or exhaling. Those who watched declared that this God/man is dead. Since some crowd folk had doubt of His death, a guard approached the plural/God's body on the timbers of wood. Here the guard pulled out a long sharp-edged sword and slowly pierced the chest cavity and out came a massive amount of blood with no body movement. Blood, blood and more blood poured all over His lower half of His body. The blood pouring onto the timbers of wood and earth below. His body confirmed dead by the guard.

Removing plural/God's body from the rough, burly, splintery, bloody wood timbers was done by two guardsmen. Untying the blood-filled ropes, pulling out the rusty, bloody nails from His body was done as He lies horizontal on the ground. Now confirmed dead, His body was placed in a grave to decay. Most criminals who received this death sentence when pronounced dead were placed openly into a huge earth hole where worms and animals would feast.

The government of that day placed this plural/God's body into a tombstone grave alone. His body was placed inside a tomb lying on the earth. The only entrance was now covered by a huge, round stone. Several guardsmen were ordered to watch the entrance of the tomb. Twenty-four hours a day the guards would watch this tomb and the crowds who gathered there. The government, crowd of people, and family and some of His closest believers knew His (God's) fate. His fate would be slowly decaying inside the sealed tomb. Many came to visit the tomb to show their grief, disbelief and sadness. Each visit, guards were there guarding the only entrance. During this time of this government history, **"no guards"** ever left their post because their consequences would be their death!

On the third day's visit to the sealed grave tomb marks in history, today, an occurrence that has been told for hundreds and thousands of years.

While visiting the tombstone on the third day, a miracle happened! (A miracle by this definition is an occurrence that could only happen if this plural/God would allow it to happen by Him.) The miracle was eye witnessed by a crowd of people gathering to the grave tomb and they observed behind the guards the tombstone was open. The huge, round stone, possibly eight feet in diameter (only approximating) was rolled a distance that the entire interior of the tomb was viewed by the crowd.

At first glance the visitors (several) in number, the guards (several) in number were all in shock, amazed that an occurrence like this occurred! The guards viewed the inside of the daylight tomb and claimed, "The body is gone." A woman entered the inside of the tomb with tears from her eyes and a grief look saw only a blanket, the body was gone! Then suddenly a voice within the tomb from an angelic spirit proclaimed to the women: "Cry not, fear not, grieve not, for He has risen. <u>Up from the grave He arose</u>!" The women viewing the angelic spirit who (temporarily took on a human body) spoke and said, "<u>Go into town, there you will find Him</u>."

In town the women found an uproar of people searching for this plural/God who escaped from the tomb! Many thought He (God) was never put in the grave tomb. Many knew His dead body was placed inside the tomb. Many thought He (God) was still in the grave tomb. Many knew the grave tomb was empty. Many thought in the middle of the night the guards took and hid the body. Many knew guards never left their post. Many thought He (God) was never dead. Many knew no one ever got off those timbers of wood alive. Many thought His closest followers bribed the guards and took His body from within the tomb. Many knew the falsehood of that bribe. Many do not believe that He (God) raised Himself to life on the third day of His death. Many believed in that day He (God) raised Himself from death to life because they saw Him. Greater are those to believe that He (God) raised Himself from the dead to life who have not seen Him. Your will! Will? Believe or not believe, that's the question?

The woman's encounter with the risen plural/ God is now on her mind. She's now proclaiming to all what she saw, touched, heard and talked to. First to find the eleven or twelve of His closest followers to tell them the good news! These closest followers, "all" of which had a personal fellowship with Him (God).

The woman's first hope of finding these closest companions was to look locally in town. There she found a few. A brief conversation took place with much doubt and disbelief among the men. Seeing is believing, the men told the woman. The woman took the chosen few followers back in her footsteps, then they found the risen God/man.

The men noticing this man who semi-looked like their God. This man had a glorified risen body which they had some doubt. As they all got closer they talked, listened to, touched and watched that He is who He said He is. The conversations that came forth from this plural/risen/God made believers of the men except for one. One of His closest followers said, "Please let me see and touch your wrists and side where the insertions were." God/man said Come close, see and feel the healed wounds. He said, "My Lord/God, thank you, I now believe." Several days had passed (only estimating) until all of His closest followers were back together as a complete unit.

Prior to this plural/God's death and now for the next thirty days (only estimating) He (God) with His closest followers began to teach, teach others to teach, preach, instruct others to preach that the "kingdom" of God is now at hand. Word got back to the government and most of the nonbelievers in Him, so that they are now getting reorganized to seize Him.

For the next thirty days His believers saw miracles after miracles. The ultimate miracle that He (God) displayed is that He raised Himself from death to life. **"Out from the grave He arose**!" Many of the dead, those who had no sight, they that had no limbs, a frail body, diseased skin and many other infirmities became fully healed when He (God) spoke words to cure them. His closest followers and other believers in Him (God) using His name and their words cured others in the same manner.

The government, the nonbelievers, and the demonic evil spirits carried on their mission to recapture this plural/God but failed.

The ultimate miracle by this plural/God was about to take place and be witnessed by only a few of His closest followers. He (God) would begin to speak to his closest followers as they all gathered around the supper table. "I must go," He said, "I must go to my Father's (God's) house. When I do go, I will prepare a place for you and all those believers in me. Where I am you will (not maybe) be also."

In my Father's house there are many mansions (currently under construction) (earth time two thousand years in the making) where there is only peace, angelic spirits, saved human spirits, my Father and myself. His followers of strong belief said, No! Don't go! These believers believed that another bloody, terror death would be on Him again. His speaking with them continued with joyful thoughts that His spirit would be (not maybe) within themselves. He explained a complete outline of earthly future events (revelations) will happen while he (God) is gone. The cheerfulness of all who heard now understood their mission (which they accept) (until this very day). Upon the thirty days (only estimating) His glorified body was ascending upward toward the uttermost distance of the sky. This crystallization of His body was crystallizing as His body vertically went upward out of sight.

CHAPTER FIFTEEN

GOD'S (PLURAL) FOUR JUDGMENTS

✝

S hortly after the beginning in the most heavenly place known was the **first judgment**. The beginning (exact date not recorded, not important) marks the first judgment of God's created angelic spirits. This judgment was for rebelling against Him, His nature, His truths, His being and influencing other created angelic spirits to do the same. At this time a spiritual war began.

This spiritual war currently enforce with a judgment from Him (plural Gods). The judgment (first known) was for all evil, demonic, sin in bound angelic spirits. These rebellion angelic spirits were cast out of the most high heavenly place where their Creator dwells. Cast out where? And why? They were sent to Planet Earth! Only one of these angelic spirit beings can travel back to the edges of the most high heavenly place for brief conversation with His Creator.

Sounds confusion? Answer yes! The why part of this spiritual war needs to be fully understood, which is simple. This eternal, holy, spirit, plural (God) wants from His spiritual creations their free will love returned back to Himself. This God feeds you, protects you, sustains you, created you for Himself. He (God) is currently preparing for the saved eternal human spirits, a mansion in the new heaven where He'll (God) dwell. This God (plural) has prepared, already completed, currently enforced, presently occupied, filling in occupancy daily a place for the fallen angelic spirits and the unsaved human spirits, a torture, fiery, sinful place of the mind, body and spirit labeled <u>eternal existence</u>. This first judgment occurred in the most high heavenly place where only angelic spirits dwells. The spiritual war is now here on Planet Earth (approximately four to five thousand years in time) and the human race is in the middle of the battlefield. Both spirits (demonic) and (holy) want their selection for all eternity. Your will! Will?

The **second judgment** from this holy, eternal, spirit God is for all nations on Planet Earth. All nations will be and currently are being judged by blessings or by the wrath of God. (Sounds unfair?) Possibly! Remembering God's ways, not demon angelic ways.

Truths vs. lies are found on all nations. Some nations in times past were consumed by fire, not a person left! This wrath by fire was God's judgment for the human race who rebel and choose other gods than Him. For it is written, "I am a jealous God, have no other gods besides Me." Other nations in times past were consumed by famine (no food) for rebelling against their Creator. The entire earth – people, all land areas – were engulfed in a flood, were judged by this plural God. These flood waters continued until all was gone! Those judgments by this plural/God are found in written form and have been proclaimed for thousands of years. Some people claim it, others claim it not! Floods, fires, diseases, crimes, government corruption, weather storms, unnatural disasters, and all other demonic, evil angelic spirit attacks on all nations are enforced. Most judgments are occurring with pre-warnings to avoid them! Others are not. Spiritual life is eternal here and at the hereafters.

The **third judgment** from text of old is for the human race only! "Once you die then a judgment" from this plural/God. Sounds fair? Right? Honest? Just? Justice? Unjust? Who Decides? Many and more questions could ponder oneself but a fact is a fact, "Once you die then the judgment." This is a true story which began in time and space on the first day on Planet Earth for the human race. This judgment occurs for the entire human race with no boundaries. **Warning**! **Warnings** and more **warnings** are known. His words, eyewitnesses, material evidence, dates, times, places and profound statements from this plural/God, that all spirits will be judged by Him and Him alone.

This plural/God states with His words, "All things material and spiritual" were created by Me. Since this is true and that other gods exists, you could believe why this God is a jealous God. Upon death (for the human race only) a judgment occurs (possibly within a second). This judgment for the unsaved human spirits who enter eternal existence know two things: there is "wailing and gnashing of teeth" (twenty-four-seven) and why they are there! The reason "why" is true for all spirits that dwell there. Reason being they (the occupants of eternal existence) rejected accepting the free gift of eternal life from the holy plural/God. There are many gods that do exist (and there are many) only one offers "freely" eternal life. By definition the word eternal is best described as: will last forever. Life is described as those who dwell there will be there forever.

The **fourth judgment** from this plural/God is for (the unsaved human spirits only) called the great, white throne judgment. Here all the unsaved human spirits will be judged by their Creator. This will be the trial of the century. No attorneys, no jurors, no eyewitnesses will be in the courtroom! Each unsaved human spirit will answer the call oneself. The brief (possibly under a second in time) remembering (there will be no time clocks) statements, opening arguments will be heard then the judgment to all who enter. Each unsaved human spirit will hear the guilty verdict of their spirit. The gavel will "bang" and the judge (plural/God) will sentence each to eternal existence. This trial will be on a case by case basis. The sentences all will remain the same to enter eternal existence. The great, white throne trial and judgment will be the **shortest** (time-wise) but will receive the **longest** (sentence-wise) to eternal existence. The most painful sentence of guilty known to the human race begins the moment of arriving.

The sentence of (lying in a lake of fire) always remembering (for eternity) the judgment, times past on Planet Earth and rejecting the "free gift" from the holy, eternal, spirit, plural/God. The unsaved human spirits at this judgment receive their sentence of eternal existence where there are **no appeals**!

Why, where and when will this judgment occur? The where will be at the outermost atmospheric spiritual place. This is where angelic spirits reside. When will this occur? When the saved and unsaved human spirits are known for the holy, eternal, spirit, God. At this time and year of history, it's getting sooner rather than later for this last judgment. Why will this last judgment occur? God's ways vs. Planet Earth god ways, truths vs. lies, darkness vs. light, blessing vs. curses, peace vs. corruption, eternal life or eternal existence. **Your will! Will?**

This plural/God needs to talk to each individual human spirit who is at this last judgment for the last time. The conversation will know who they were (past tense), how they lived, what they did, when they chose Planet Earth god, why they were created and how they could have escaped this white throne judgment.

CHAPTER SIXTEEN

LIFE WITH PLURAL/ GOD – PAST, PRESENT AND FUTURE

✝

Life (by this definition is) your spirit will live forever with Him (plural God). Sounds confusing? Sounds impossible? Sounds unrealistic? Sounds undeserving? Sounds like your "free will" needs to choose "eternal life" where there is a mansion being prepared for all human spirits that believe in Him! Why? Continue to read on...

Life with this eternal God is "why" He came to Planet Earth. He (God) "came into the world the usual way." This (plural/God) wrote a text of old day (currently being read today) so that you can have (not maybe) salvation with Him. This text of old day (approximately a few thousand years old) is the number one best seller known to the human race. This text explains: how to live, who to live with, why you're living, when you're going to die, where you're going after you die, who to believe in, who not to believe in, and the only purpose of why you were born! This text is found on all continents, written in most all languages known to man. Belief is now known that this (plural/God) is trying to reach out to all.

People in times past have believed in this plural/God, received the free "gift" of eternal life and are now with Him forever in eternal paradise! Those whose bodies are now dead, buried in the ground, in the depths of the water or scattered in the air and have believed are all with Him. Their bodies all have (past tense) returned to the earth (whence they came). Their spirits have (present tense) returned to Him (plural/God) who created them. This sequence of events is currently happening today. "**Today is the day of salvation**."

A man once spoke during his "heyday" on Planet Earth, "There's nothing new under the sun." This speaking occurred four to five thousand years ago (only estimating). The human race today can have a personal relationship with this plural/God. Remembering "many are called but few are chosen" to accept this free gift of eternal life. Eternal life begins here on Planet Earth when accepting Him. The human spirit is saved from eternal existence. This could be described as a miracle. The human spirit within the body will last forever; your free will determines where: **eternal life or eternal existence**.

Eternal life or eternal existence begins here on Planet Earth by having only two choices: from darkness to light, from unrighteousness to righteousness, from deception to truth, then you'll know where you're going, why you're going, who will be going, and those not going! Going where? Entering a no time zone of eternal life. Where there are no thieves, robbers, quackery, adulterers, fornicators, lovers of themselves and absolutely no wrongs. Simply perfection of all who reside there, as He (God) is. At this time of acceptance you are on the winning side of this spiritual war. You now can talk to this (plural/God) and ask anything. The answers will be provided, then you'll know, what now you don't.

Life with (plural/God's) future is savings the best for last, which will be for eternity. **Don't "worry" be "happy"** at eternal life, known as a place where you'll have a new name, new body, same spirit. What to do at eternal life? One must compare eternal life with: Planet Earth! Or eternal existence! From first knowledge there's a lot to compare: at Planet Earth there is a demonic, satanic, evil spirit god. This god is mostly in control of all things with little limitations. This demonic earth god has a multitude of evil, spiritual angelic angels doing the same toward this plural/God's human race creation.

Whatever this plural/God can do, this demonic earth god believes he can do better. The host of evil spirits is huge! The exact number unknown to the human race. What is known about this demonic force is that: (one-thousand) demonic spirits can enter the human body. Once entered they (demonic spirits) can take over the body and mind of that person. This person when trapped demonically is out of control of his normal bodily functions and mind. This happening is occurring more than not on Planet Earth.

Comparing plural/God's eternal spirit life with eternal existence, one can note the similarities and differences. Both are the same; as both will always know why they are there! Both will (not maybe) last for eternity. Both will remember (plural/God's) name for eternity. Both have **no exits, no returns**.

The differences are huge in number; many spirits will occupy eternal existence compared to a few entering eternal life. Just punishments will be the fate of those who dwell in eternal existence where rewards and comfort for those of eternal life. One will have the same name, same body. The other will receive a new name and a new body. One will continue to thirst and hunger, the other will eat and drink. Some spirits will continue to thank, praise, honor and glorify their Creator. The plentiful spirits will curse their Creator. One area of eternity will have only inchly movements (opinion only). The other spirits will travel to the new heaven, new earth, new galaxies, planets and stars faster than a blink of an eye. One will have close-knit boundaries. The others will continue to explore a no-time, space zone. One will be burning of the body while lying on a lake of fire. The other spirits will receive comfort by their Creator. One will know a limit of why things happened to themselves. The others will know why all things happen. Both will know the demonic, satanic, evil spiritual war is over with sentences for eternity.

Life with this plural/God's future is happening now on Planet Earth. It's happening only for the human race spirits who believe in Him and why He came. These are foolish thoughts for those who don't believe! All human spirit animals have what no other animals have, which is two-fold. The first is a free will (best definition) to choose right from wrong, good from evil to determine a destiny of eternal life or eternal existence. The second is the human race has within their body a spirit. A spirit (best definition) will last for eternity and you decide where your spirit will reside. Life, future with this plural/God is only for those human spirits who have trust in Him while they were living on Planet Earth. **This is the only entrance requirement**. No test to take, no good works to do, only having a belief in this plural/God. Sounds too good to be true? Well, it is!

Life with this plural/God is for eternity. What does this really mean? Much is unknown. What is known for all of his saved human spirits is that He (God) is preparing a place for them where He resides. Pondering about this statement one could consider this: the earth and all of its settings was created by Him in six earth days. What a marvel! In six twenty-four hours days what you see, feel, touch, hear and all that you can't was created by this plural/God. Of all the (gods) that do exist (and there are many) **none has ever made such a claim as this plural/God has**.

Life future with this God for all eternity, this is known; no need to sleep because no one will get tired. No need to be in the dark because all will be light. No need to work as everything will be provided. No thoughts of evil or corruption, only truth will prevail.

No remembrance of Planet Earth, "Behold all things become new." No races of people. No nine to five work schedule as no paychecks are needed. No males or females, no young or old, no weak or strong, all who reside will be one as He is one.

Where to go? What to do? Who will be there? Why will only a few human spirits be there? How you'll travel? And why eternal life? Where to go at eternal life much is known! Everything will become new: new heaven, earth, planets, galaxies and mansions (one per person) at eternal life settings. There will be a new way of traveling (without using energy)! To and fro heaven's destinations, just like angelic spirits do. This form of travel is a mystery not completely known because this way of moving is not practiced by the human race. Traveling faster than the speed of light (remembering there's no sunlight in the new heaven), traveling faster than a speeding bullet (remembering no guns will be allowed), traveling through material things like floors, walls, ceilings, planets, galaxies, solar systems and other objects will be a common practice of all spiritual residents in eternal life. A greater mystery and understanding is for the human spirits only as they will be able to stand and observe all things in their travels. The human spirits will have a new body at eternal life. Your spirit will be the same one given to you on Planet Earth. Sounds confusion? Answer yes! Sounds impossible, answer no! With this high speed of travel one could ponder, what to do when you get to each destination? One answer would be that you can walk to and fro on arrival. There will be plenty of drink and food to consume. The food and drink costs nothing, no cooks to cook (already prepared), no cleanup, no mess and plenty for all! What can the occupants do who reside in eternal life? Say thanks! to this plural/God for His gift.

Traveling with this holy, eternal, plural/God, and asking a multitude of questions (probably some questions you're thinking of right now) will be answered as you go. This traveling will be talk and walk with Him (God) while standing or through wide open heavenly places.

Who will be at eternal life in the new heaven? The answer is three-fold. First, the one, true, holy, eternal spirit, plural/God will be there as this is His dwelling place. Second, the non-rebellious angelic spirits will be there (remembering these spirits have no bodies). Their quest in eternal life is to serve their Creator and the human race body spirits. Third, those who dwell there were taken by "a man who claims to be God" on Planet Earth. This taking was done by all people who with their "free will" accepted God's grace and His free gift of eternal life. The total number of human spirits (daily increasing) who will dwell there is not known at this day of history and therefore is not important. What is known of the human spirits of Planet Earth is that they will all know each other at eternal life. Trying to understand that these happenings are happening takes only faith. Faith in who? and Why? The only answer is faith in this plural/spirit/God. Why? Having **faith is the only entrance requirement**!

The human spirits of Planet Earth who have gained entrance in eternal life will know the names of all other residents there. Wow! From an earthly perspective it's difficult to accept because of our limitations. Remembering the residents of eternal life will be like He (plural/God) is. Since He knows all names of planets, stars, angelic and human spirits, those who dwell there will know the same. Imagine knowing all individual names of the residents of eternal life! The human spirits will have a new name (one per person), a new body (not male or female), and will know everything there. The residents' names there will be no two alike. One could believe (millions or billions) of individual names of eternal spirits will be there. These names are already known and will be told to all those human spirits who reside there by this (plural, spirit, eternal/God).

Why is this plural/God doing what He is doing? One could ponder and say, "I don't know." These "doings" have been (past tense) in the "making" prior to the creation of Planet Earth.

Love from this plural/God is shown and has been shown to all He (God) encounters. (He) having the **"power,"** **which self-sustains Himself is a "marvel"** to be told again, again and again. This "marvel" was first displayed to all the angelic spirits in the first heaven. One-third of these angelic spirits chose not to completely accept His love gift. The "free will" of these one-third angelic spirits chose evil toward their Creator and today, thus remain the same. The human race spirits were created next and are second in line to accept this marvel of love from their Creator. One could now believe this plural/God is trying to reach out for the human race. His love is shown from the air you breathe, the food you eat, material things you have, your talents bestowed upon you and the eternal love gift from a "man who claims to be God." The only entrance requirement to enter eternal life.

This plural, spirit/God is a God who's always working. At this time of Planet Earth history this "God" is preparing a place for all those human spirits that have faith in Him. Faith is all this plural/God asks.

The "why" part of this equation is a mystery to all mankind who have put their trust of eternal life with Him. Since He (plural/God) has conquered death, "Death where is thou sting," it is written, "Once you die then the judgment," it makes sense to believe.

CHAPTER SEVENTEEN

ETERNAL LIFE OR
ETERNAL EXISTENCE
YOUR WILL

O f all the names of God (and there are many) there is only one name given among the human race whereby you must be saved. This statement (very bold) in nature! Not if you think it's a good thing to do or something just to think about, rather than a statement of fact. You must be saved! Saved from what? Answer is: eternal existence. These writings were written more than two thousand years ago. It is true, those living back then (must be saved) from a horrific place of eternal torture, just like today. This is found from one of the oldest texts known to the human race. This preserved text is (possibly) one of the oldest books known and was the first book printed in the English language. God has reached the human race by his written words: **BEWARE**! You must be saved from eternal existence. This place is secluded, you're all alone, you chose not to accept His free gift of eternal life. "Many are called but few are chosen."

The human race spirits with their intact eternal spirit must be saved. From what? The what is now known. The what will last for eternity. The what will be a just punishment. The what will be: eternal torture of the mind, body and spirit. This torture will be a total separation of all that you knew and a complete separation from your Creator.

The where? is described by: a place, an actual setting, a secluded no-time zone. Where there will be yelling and shouting with such a high degree of pain and suffering for all who dwell there. This torture is described by "wailing and gnashing of teeth," the "skin slowly burning," "little or no movement," drink not, sleep not, exit not. Think yes, talk yes, remember yes, complain yes. These happenings happen in days past, today, and will happen in future days.

This name given to the human race spirits, whereby, "you must be saved," separated B.C. from A.D. The prophecy occurred exactly as it was fore-told for centuries. **Now God is among us**. He (God) now can be seen, heard, touched and examined that He is who He said He is without deceptions. This text approximately a few thousand years old (only estimating) contains one-fourth prophecies all about Him (God). Prophecies of who, what, where, why and how come which describes everything. Everything such as what happened in the beginning, what is happening now and what is happening in the future.

Religions, religions and more religions! In excess of fifteen hundred (only estimating) with gods, gods and more gods are found. This God (plural in nature) has (past tense) prepared a path for the saved human spirits which is straight and narrow. The Planet Earth god prepared a path which is broad and huge which leads to total destruction while living on Planet Earth. This broad road leads the human spirit into eternal existence, where many chose and choose this route. This narrow path is plain and simple because you are to follow Him. His words now found only in print, describe the first from the last and which direction your "free will" will choose.

The broad road of destruction begins the moment of birth and can continue one's entire life. Destruction (by this definition) is: sin, incurring wrongs, lies, and/or creating a personal relationship only with the god of Planet Earth. Earthly and eternal destruction continues (without end) by not accepting a "**free gift**" (one that no one deserves) from this plural/God. Destruction of the body, mind, spirit, family, spouse, oneself, business, education, pleasure, lust, adultery, greed, money, envy, covetousness, lovers of thyself and all others this earth god can offer. Rapidly, rapidly a lifetime passes by without a personal relationship with this plural/God. Death occurs for this nonbeliever then enters eternal existence.

Now comes eternal life starting here on Planet Earth for the human spirits only. This occurs for those human spirits who (all who choose) put their faith and trust in this plural/God. At this moment, giving your sins to this plural/God and in return receive forgiveness here on earth and when your spirit leaves the body (upon death) enters eternal life.

What an opportunity for all. Only one lifetime to choose this opportunity. This opportunity is for the human spirits, because we are made in His image. Eternal life for the human race begins on a moment's notice of giving Him (plural/God) your sins, wrongs, adultery, lies and your boundness toward this earth god, surname "Devil". In return you'll receive eternal life only for your spirit. **Remember you are a spirit who has temporarily taken on a human body**. The spirit will continue for eternity, depending only upon where? Eternal existence or eternal life.

How do you know you're saved? "Behold all things become new." A fresh start with the ending being the best (entering eternal life). Sounds unbelievable! Sounds undeserving! Sounds better than eternal existence? Yes! Knowing that you're saved from (eternal existence) is a gift of grace from this plural God. Faith in Him is the only entrance requirement to enter. This faith is the substance of evidences sometimes unseen but still believed.

The evidences of being saved are many; reading more about this man who claims to be God, watching miracles which are currently occurring and being with others who are doing the same. Some of your sins will vanish. Some of your wrongdoings will occur no more. You'll be the best evidence you're saved! Your sins as you pass through life are many (possibly), too many to name. No need to remember those sins that are in your midst, because all are buried deeper than the deepest part of the ocean. Never to curse the entrance of eternal life, having faith of this (plural/God) who has the only key. You'll know, and others will know most sins are gone from your life and all sins been redeemed by the blood of this (plural/God). This is why this God (plural in nature) was born to die and rise again (bodily) on the third day for the (human race) spirits only to believe in Him for eternal life.

This man who claims to be God was given a name (above every name) at His birth. Leaving eternal heaven where the first spiritual war began and shortly ended, He (God) came to earth and was born from a virgin woman. This miracle birth was one of His earliest miracles among the many He had witnessed during His earthly life. The spiritual war is over at eternal heaven, however the second phase of this spiritual war is huge! This spiritual war is in full force here on Planet Earth. This plural/God came to earth to put an end to this spiritual war. The end of this war is now known, where the demonic, evil, satanic, rebelling angelic spirits, unsaved human spirits and the Planet Earth god will enter eternal existence.

These fallen evil, demonic, rebelling angelic spirits (first created) in eternal heaven were cast out to Planet Earth. How many? Not known, not important to know. What is known is that a thousand of these evil spirits can enter an unsaved human spirit. That's power!

This plural/God was given a name (from birth) on Planet Earth that is spoken in more languages than any other name. **A name greater than any other god's name**! Only His name has an open, unrestricted, invitation to come... to Him (God) for your entrance to eternal life in heaven. Those who call (human spirits only) upon him, He'll no wise cast out. Cast out to where? <u>Eternal existence</u>, where the worms dieth not and feed on their captures. Will there be hungry, bloodthirsty, crawling, slimy worms that eat their prey in eternal existence? Answer... yes!

This plural/God spoke, and wrote more about His wrath toward His created human spirits compared to his "love" for them. **The human race was born an enemy of God**. A text was written about this plural/God thousands of years ago. This text consists of sixty-six books, was and is copied and copied more times over thousands of years than any other text of its origin. Without error! The "number one" book that has and is selling the most than any other book of all time is this one. If one cannot afford this text to buy, many organizations, companies, places of worship will provide it at no cost. On every continent, country, province, town, city and rural land areas this plural/God's book or knowledge of Him is found. Compared to other gods this magnitude is not there. The chapters of this text and the words written is to have (present tense) salvation with Him.

Salvation is found only through this plural/God's birth name. As it is written thousands of years ago (only estimating), "There is no other name given among the human race spirits whereby we must be saved." Such a bold convincing statement! Made by no other God. **Such a warning!** Such a profound acknowledgement! Such a truth! There is no other salvation by any other god to enter eternal heaven for the human race spirits. This is the only entrance requirement. Remembering: everything was created by Him (plural/God), everything material was designed by Him. Every spirit, animal (known and unknown), every planet, galaxy, universe, star, occupied and unoccupied spaces were created for Him and by Him.

You have been selected by this plural/God to be born at this day and time in history on Planet Earth. Everything you know about yourself and most that you don't know was designed by Him for His honor and glory. Now you know that you have (present tense) been selected by Him for the only purpose of your life. This purpose will (not maybe) determine your destiny. Remembering the human body will return to the earth whence it came. Your spirit will return to the holy, eternal, spirit, plural/God who created it! This returning of the spirit will be for both spirits: the spirit that believes in him (God) to enter eternal life (the only entrance requirement necessary). The other non-believing spirit when it leaves its human body will return to its maker. Both spirits will have a brief conversation with their Creator; one will enter eternal existence where the body and spirits lie in fire. the other believing spirit enters eternal life where they are now in comfort. Both dwelling eternal where there are **no exits**.

Songs, **songs** and more **songs** were written about this plural/God than any other god. Some of these songs written and sung by those of old days. How many years ago? Four to five thousand years (only estimating). So, songs were sung to this plural/God who the people never saw, only heard His voice. Thousands, thousands and thousands of songs have been written and sung about this plural/God. In the twenty first century the number one song about this plural/God that sold the most copies and is sung the most is "**Amazing Grace**."

Among the different languages spoken there are many songs found about this plural/God. Some of these songs are about who He is, why He is, and what an opportunity He (God) has provided for the human race spirits. From some of the oldest books known, to those books of the 21st century, more songs have been written to honor and glorify this plural/God.

These songs cross all the major language barriers. On all continents where the human race dwells songs are sung to and about this individual plural/God every day (twenty-four-seven) at places of worship, homes, in automobiles, all transportation vehicles, those who walk, those who are bedridden and many others, sing, listen to songs about this plural/God than any other god in history. Instruments like the harp (of old day), flute, piano, drums, guitar, banjo, and more music of the twenty first century have been used to honor and glorify this holy, eternal, spirit, God. The words written within these songs (mostly) tell a story of this plural/God: "**How great thou art**."

Books, books and more books have been written, are currently being written about this plural/God than any other god. This great, almighty, highest, holy, truthful, eternal, spirit God wrote (using the human race hands and pen) the number one book about Himself consisting of sixty-six chapters! This book, written over a few thousand years, describes everything about the past, present and future happenings for the human race spirits. This book is without error! This book, written by many different authors, many who never knew the other. The subject matter of these writings is one-fourth prophecy. Prophecy (by this definition is) information that will come to pass as it is detailed, prior to its happening. These sixty-six chapters describe: prophecy, prophecy and more prophecy that has been, is, and will be fulfilled as it has been foretold; soon it will be over for the human race to enter eternal existence or eternal life.

The remaining three-fourths of this text details a spiritual war between two eternal spirits. (Remembering a spirit you cannot see with the human eye.) Spirits can see other spirits and material things. Spirits can speak, reason, think, ponder, do good, or enter evil, corrupt, sins against their Creator. This spiritual war is between a holy, eternal, everlasting Creator of all things material, spiritual and a created spirit and a host of evil, demonic angelic spirits.

How many evil, demonic spirits are there? (Not known, not important.) Are all these evil spirits totally against their Creator spirit? Yes! (Possibly) a trillion "plus" demonic, angelic spirits waging war against one everlasting, eternal spirit. The odds look "dim" toward the one, holy, eternal spirit compared to the trillions (only estimating) evil host spirits (which are created spirits), until you know all the facts. "I want the facts, the whole facts and nothing but the facts," has been foretold here on Planet Earth for centuries.

CHAPTER EIGHTEEN

<u>TITLES AND PERSONAL NAMES OF GOD</u>

<u>PERSONAL NAMES OF GOD</u>

<u>LEGION</u> – For we are many.

<u>ELOHIM</u> – Plurality in unity.

<u>EL</u> – As to His power. He is Almighty God.

<u>ELAH</u> – Hebrew verb meaning to fear, to worship, to adore.

<u>ELOAH</u> – The only living and true God.

<u>EL ELYON</u> – God most high.

<u>EL-ROI</u> – The Lord that seeth.

<u>EL-ELOHE-ISRAEL</u> – God of Israel.

<u>EL-OLAM</u> – God of eternity. The everlasting God.

<u>ADON-ADONAI</u> – Jehovah our ruler. An intensive plural of Adon, meaning "Lord," expressing divine dominion.

<u>JAH</u> – The independent one. Is a short form of Jehovah. The present living God.

159

JEHOVAH – I am that I am: self-existing one. The eternal, everlasting one.

JEHOVAH-ELOHIM – Majestic omnipotent God.

JEHOVAH-HOSEENU – The Lord our maker.

JEHOVAH-JIREH –The Lord will provide.

JEHOVAH-ROPHI – The Lord, the physician.

JEHOVAH-NISSI – The Lord our banner.

JEHOVAH-M'KADDESH – The lord doth sanctify; to obey, purity to God, to healthiness, to diet, to instruct, remember, to the hallowed soul and to the hallowed body.

JEHOVAH-ELOHEENU – Lord our God.

JEHOVAH SHALOM — The Lord our peace.

JEHOVAH-TSEBAOTH – The Lord of hosts.

JEHOVAH-TSIDKENU – The Lord our righteousness.

JEHOVAH-MAKKEH – The Lord shall smite thee.

JEHOVAH-GMOLAH – The God of recompenses.

JEHOVAH-SHAMMAH – The Lord is there.

FATHER – Distinguishing title of God. The Creator of all spirits.

FATHER OF SPIRITS – The God of the spirits of all flesh.

FATHER OF LIGHTS – The light of the natural world, the sun, moon, the stars shining in the heavens; the light of reason and conscience; the light of His laws.

FATHER OF GLORY – The king of glory.

MY FATHER – The pronoun of personal possession.

YOUR FATHER – A divine name of God of eternal heaven.

<u>OUR FATHER</u> – Our father in heaven. God's dwelling place.

<u>HOLY FATHER</u> – Describes God's nature of being divine.

<u>RIGHTEOUS FATHER</u> – Describes God's truths.

<u>ABBA FATHER</u> – Jewish prayer of which God was addressed; Lord of all the earth.

<u>GOD OF HEAVEN</u> – Divine. His dwelling place above.

<u>JEALOUS GOD</u> – God of solicitude for truth.

<u>CHRIST</u> – The Son of the Father. The Son of the living God. The righteous one. Jesus, the prophet of Nazareth.

<u>SON</u> – Jesus born of the flesh. The Son of the Father.

<u>SPIRIT</u> – Everlasting, holy God.

<u>EMMANUEL</u> – God with us.

<u>I'AM</u> – I'am that I'am declares God the resurrection and the life.

<u>LORD</u> – The same as holy, eternal, everlasting God.

<u>CREATOR</u> – Lord God who creates all things spiritual and material.

<u>ALPHA AND THE OMEGA</u> – Is the first and the last. The beginning and the end.

<u>SAVIOR</u> – The savior Jesus the Christ of God.

<u>ALMIGHTY</u> – God which is, and which was, and which is to come.

<u>TITLES OF GOD</u>

The God of Bethel, the Lord and Judge of All the Earth. God of Abraham, Isaac and of Jacob. The Rock of His Salvation. The Sword of Excellency. The

Lord and the Judge. The Lord of Hosts. Lord God of Heaven. The Great, the Mighty and Terrible God. Maker, Holy One, Preserver of Men, the Almighty. The Lord's Anointed, My King, Man, Head of Heathen, Seed of David, the Lord Strong and Mighty. Thy Servant and the Righteous One. The Headstone of the Corner. The Shepherd. Lord of Lords. The Redeemer. The Ring. The Judge. The Lawgiver. King of Heaven. God of Heaven. The Great God. God of Gods. The Most High God. The Lord God of Hosts. Tower of the Flock. A God Like Unto Thee. Lord of Whole Earth. God of Judgment. Great King. Father-Creator. The Lord Changing Not.

TITLES AND PERSONAL NAMES
OF GOD THE SON

ADAM – The man Christ Jesus, who came as "the last Adam"

ANOINTED – Hebrew word; Messiah.

APOSTLE – Means "one sent forth".

ARM OF THE LORD – The Lord be revealed.

AUTHOR – The Greek word implies, "that which causes something".

BEGINNING AND END – The Lord creates the beginning of life and the end for all.

BELOVED – "My beloved" or my "sole unique Son," declares God.

BRANCH OF JEHOVAH – The Emmanuel character of Christ.

BREAD – The bread of eternal spiritual life.

BRIDEGROOM – Christ presents Himself to His own.

CAPTAIN OF OUR SALVATION – There is salvation in none other to be received by God.

CARPENTER – From family, Christ followed this trade.

CHIEF CORNERSTONE – Describes Christ as "a living stone".

CHILD – "Today" a child is born to take away the sins of the world.

CHRIST – Who is ruler over all. Sovereignty.

CONSOLATION – The "One" who they waited for.

COUNSELOR – The "One" who provides only truths.

COVENANT – The "One" who provides truths for eternal life with Him.

DAY SPRING – The "One" who "rising up" will deliver "His" truths of salvation.

DESIRE OF ALL NATIONS – The "One" who will be known of all nations, for salvation.

DELIVER – The "One" who rescues the human spirits from sin for eternal life.

DOOR – I am the only door by means of eternal life.

ELECT – The human spirits were chosen in Christ, in a past eternity, for salvation with the eternal God of heaven.

EMMANUEL – God is with us.

ENSIGN – Lord means Jehovah.

EVERLASTING FATHER – Father of eternity.

FAITHFUL AND TRUE – Christ's truthful ways.

FAITHFUL WITNESS – The "One" that gives testimony of truth.

FIRST AND THE LAST – Greek; alpha and omega. Applied to Christ as eternal and supreme.

FINISHER OF FAITH – Origin and author of faith.

FIRST BORN – Prophecy, God now with us.

FORERUNNER – Christ's life to run the life of faith in Him (God).

FOUNDATION – On Christ, the solid rock, I stand: All other ground is sinking sand.

FOUNTAIN – Of life everlasting; without end.

FRIEND – Heavenly (God) friendship came to earth to show salvation in only Himself.

GIFT OF GOD – Blessed to receive God's gift of eternal life through only His son.

GLORY – He is the Lord of glory. Heaven's declare the glory of God.

GOD – Plural names. One in nature. Jesus the Christ of God is the only God.

GOVERNOR – Christ a judge, a lawgiver.

HEAD – God; heir of all things.

HIGH PRIEST – The "One" who has unchangeable truths.

HOLY ONE – The Messiah is the Holy One eternal spirit.

HORN OF SALVATION – Indicating there is salvation with the Father (God) only through the Son, Christ.

I'AM – The Son presented Himself as Jehovah – Jesus, the only eternal spirit God of heaven.

IMAGE – Christ declares, "I am the image of God."

JESUS – Born of a virgin. Declares "I'am that I'am," JE – This first syllable Je or Jeho or Jah – Jehovah – this name of God; 2nd syllable "sus" is associated with the name Oshea, Hosea, or Houshaia, meaning "help". Jesus, "name is above every name". Jesus is God who became a man. A man who through His evidences declared He is God. Jesus was put to death when nailed to timbers of wood. Jesus was placed in a grave dead, rose from out of the grave bodily on the 3rd day, showed Himself to thousands of people and to His closest followers. "Out from the grave He arose." Jesus declared, "I am the way, the truth and the life, no one comes to the Father but by me." Jesus declares, "There is no other name given among men whereby you must be saved, saved from perishing in and at eternal existence."

JUDGE – Jesus the risen Lord from the dead, was the "One" ordained by God to be the judge of the living and the dead.

JUST ONE — This righteous "One" (God) has been unjustly tried; sentenced to death.

KING OF KINGS – This king (plural God) is the son of Jesus who reigns forever and ever.

LAMB OF GOD – Who was born to die for the sins of the world. The God-man or "God manifest in flesh.

LIFE – "I am... the life." "He that has the Son hath life."

LIGHT – He, Himself is light and no darkness. Light everlasting.

ONLY BEGOTTEN – His truths, His pre-existence and diety. He Jesus making Himself equal with God.

PASSOVER – Christ the Passover.

PHYSICIAN – Jesus the Great Physician of complete healing and for obtaining salvation for God the Father.

PLANT OF REKNOWN – The Messiah, the Christ, and Savior, which is a messianic prophecy who obtained salvation for His flock of people for eternal life.

POWER OF GOD – Christ, the power and wisdom of God.

PRINCE OF PRINCES – Declaring wisdom and power of all things material and spiritual, above all other princes.

PROPHET – His human name, Christ, His messianic name, Lord, His Jehovah name God. All were prophesied and came to pass.

RABBI – Jesus you are a rabbi, a teacher who comes from God. A reason why Jesus was put to death on timbers of wood.

LION – "The lion of the tribe of Judah." Lion indicate His resurrection on the 3rd day.

LORD – Christ's claim of equality with the Father. Christ is the Savior, the promised Messiah and the sovereign Lord of men and angels. The Greek word for Lord is Kurios, which refers to: God, Jehovah, Adon, Adonay and Elohim.

MAN – The "Man," Jesus Christ.

MASTER – The Greek word "Kurios," meaning Lord. The "One" who knows all and by Him all things were created that was created.

MEDIATOR – The "One" who acts as a guarantee to eternal life in heaven.

MESSIAH – The anointed "One," who is the son Christ Jesus.

MIGHTY GOD – One born for the salvation of this world, for eternal life, with the holy, eternal, spirit God. He sustains all things material and spiritual.

MORNING STAR – Refers to the messiahship of Our Lord for those who believe in Him.

NAZARENE – Jesus of Nazareth.

SECOND MAN – Superiority of Jesus as man is prominent, is impersonated in His true ideal as God.

SEED – This word used in the highest sense as applied to the life of God the Son. Born from a woman of the holy, eternal, spirit's seed.

SERVANT – "Christ's" mission during His life. I delight to do thy will, o my God. Jesus, voluntary submission.

SHEPHERD – The "One," who is Christ, who saves His own to enter eternal life.

SHILOH – Meaning "tranquility" or "rest". The Messiah whose reign will be one of peace and rest.

SON – Refers to "Christ as a Son" and "the Son of God's love". His Son, "Jesus Christ". The Son, "only begotten". His resurrection. The "Father" and the "Son" are one.

STAR – The prophecy of the star, as Messiah, refers to Jesus, the Christ of God.

RABBONI – This Aramaic form of rabbi, is a title of the highest dignity.

REDEEMER – The cross, on which the Prince of Glory died as our redemption.

RESURRECTION – I am the resurrection and the life.

RIGHTEOUS – The Lord "Jesus Christ," our righteousness.

ROCK – The Lord's our rock, all other is "sinking sand".

ROOT – Described the coming Messiah, "Christ" as a root of strength, wisdom and all knowledge.

ROSE – Describes His beauty and fragrance.

SANCTIFICATION – The saved "human spirits only" are sanctified from their sins and now can enter eternal life where the holy, spirit, eternal God resides.

SAVIOR – Christ was "born a Savior," "God our Savior," faith in Jesus as the only Savior for eternal life in heaven.

SCEPTRE – Symbol of authority. A prince, a king, a final lawgiver; Jesus the Christ.

WONDERFUL – An adjective meaning "marvelous." The Son proved he's wonderful by His truths and labors. "God was manifest in the flesh."

WORD – Spoken and written words declare "Christ is co-equal with God in the duration of His existence." The heart of God now revealed.

YOUNG CHILD – How early in "Jesus' life" He was persecuted. Knew all of the "wisdom" of everything without learning.

Of the many titles, personal names of the eternal, holy, spirit God and Son, there is only one name given to the human race spirits whereby you must be saved from eternal existence. This name conquered death. This birth name separated B.C. from A.D. when used in proper context toward the hosts of the demonic, evil, spirit empire, their defeat. All spirits will know this name in and at eternity. There is no other greater eternal God, spirit, Son name than this one.

This name is the most hated on Planet Earth, where only a few human spirits are elected to accept. This name holds the **only** entrance and all authority to and in eternal life. All things material and spiritual were created by this name. This name knows everything and did not have to learn anything. The way, the truth, the life to eternal heaven is by this name alone. This name self-sustains itself without energy. What to do to gain entrance into eternal existence? Nothing! **What to do to gain entrance into eternal life? By this name: Jesus the Christ of God! Your will! Will?**

<u>REFERENCES</u>

—Opinion
—Education: B.S. and M.D.
— 1611 King James, Holy Scriptures

<u>WARNING!</u>

Τhis text, "Eternal Life or Eternal Existence—
Your Will," contains graphic descriptions of
inhuman torture of the mind, body and spirit. Do
not read this text if torture, graphic descriptions of
the mind, body and spirit affects you. No words
written within this text refer to the reader, rather to
the author.

Printed in the United States
205940BV00001B/55-147/P